A Thousand Y
of East Africa

John E.G. Sutton

A Thousand Years of East Africa

British Institute in Eastern Africa
Nairobi

Published by the British Institute in Eastern Africa,
P.O. Box 30710, Nairobi, Kenya
and at Royal Geographical Society,
Kensington Gore, London SW7 2AR, U.K.

International distributor: Thames and Hudson, London

Produced in Kenya by
Initiatives Ltd.
P.O. Box 69313
Nairobi, Kenya
Tel. 340650, 505920; Fax 505920; Telex 22448

Printed by English Press Ltd.
P.O. Box 30127
Nairobi, Kenya

Reprinted 1992

Cataloguing-in-Publication Data

A thousand years of East Africa/John E.G. Sutton. – Nairobi, Kenya:
British Institute in Eastern Africa, 1990.

Bibliography: p.
Includes index

ISBN 1-872566-00-6

A Thousand Years of East Africa

Prologue

In 1986–87 the British Institute in Eastern Africa – which exists for the promotion of historical and archaeological research in this region – arranged a travelling exhibition called '500 Years Ago in East Africa'. That illustrated a selection of the results of work of the previous 25 years, and was displayed in National Museums and British Council centres in the three East African capitals and certain regional towns. It made no pretence to a comprehensive coverage – much though one would have liked to offer a convincing picture of that former age. Instead, it attempted to illustrate, by means of a set of pictorial boards and modest accompanying displays, some of the more important research and discoveries from which the cultural and economic development of this part of the world is being reconstructed.

This illustrated book is not the guide to that exhibition, but it does derive from it and shares its purpose. The change of title from '500 Years Ago' to *A Thousand Years* does not betoken a longer coverage. The former was chosen for the exhibition to help the public to focus back, though not of course on the late fifteenth century AD specifically and exclusively. But five-hundred years ago, give and take a few centuries, becomes effectively the last one-thousand years. Such a span, corresponding roughly to what is often called the later part of the Iron Age, certainly does not reach the limits of current knowledge; but it is enough to handle and is adequate for the present purpose. Again, in no way does this short book attempt to be comprehensive; it offers, rather, a selection of themes which can be illustrated by active research, mostly undertaken in the years since Independence.

History deals with change and achievement through time, and it is common for books on the subject to be arranged chronologically in order to describe a period or to explain a particular subject from its beginning, real or supposed, to its end. Some older histories, both written and remembered, which are used as sources alongside the archaeological findings in the different chapters of this book, follow that conventional form. Certain of them display an obsession with origins and with the founding of settlements and kingdoms. Time and again on opening such studies at chapter 1 we learn in clear and confident terms about the 'first' king, or about the 'first man to come to the land of . . .', or indeed about the descent of the first cattle from the sky, or the planting of the first banana, or whatever has been central to that people's livelihood and ideology.

It happens that many modern historians choose to follow this traditional model by trying to begin at the 'beginning'. In this book a different approach is preferred, one which takes the present as its reference and probes backwards. In doing this we do not pretend to get everything right, but we attempt to identify some themes of modern relevance in ancient, and not so ancient, history. At the same time this approach should assist us in controlling the varied historical sources, traditional and ethnographic and even linguistic, to ask new questions of them and to frame the next round of research enquiries. By rejecting a simple chronological progression, we do not wish to throw dating to the winds. On the contrary, any advance in our understanding of the development of East African populations requires a fuller chronology and demands that we sort our expanding information of people, events and developments into the right order. But a tyranny of historical 'facts' and lists of dates are of little use to either students or the public.

This needs to be stressed because History is a matter of public concern, being educational in the broadest sense, not simply a subject for school and university syllabuses. It is the narrowly didactic, frequently moralising way in which it is often taught (and even examined) which emasculates it intellectually and brings the subject into contempt. All too commonly we encounter a concern for 'true' or 'correct' history or we read letters in the newspapers complaining that the history of this district or of that 'tribe' has been 'miswritten'. The good news here is that History matters to these people, enough to arouse passions as keenly as do politics and religion. Such enthusiasm can, once controlled, serve as the base for rational argument and new enquiries, which in turn should lead to more attractive and informative teaching and lecturing, as well as better books and press coverage of the subject. Of course historians must strive for accuracy of facts, but these are only the building materials not the object of the enquiry. One historical 'authority' may be better than none, but better still are two contrasting approaches which can be debated and correlated thus to stimulate new questions, new research.

A more refined line of objection is to identify – or vilify – the sources used as unreliable or 'biased'. But that is the nature of the whole game; all historical sources are of necessity biased, and the historian who *believes* his sources is not worth his salt. It is what he can get from them, what he can read between the lines and deduce from the conflicts of evidence which the varied biases present, that produces historical understanding worth the effort.

The notion that it is possible to obtain a 'true' or 'complete' history – as if it be a matter of faith rather than enquiry – is an especially insidious one. It encourages the supposition that not far ahead we shall have the 'final' word, the logical corollary of which would be that knowledge is finite and that we shall soon reach the end of the road and be able to relax from our explorations and endeavours till eternity. Such scholastic deception, if not simple academic laziness, shuts the door to real research and intellectual discussion; at the same time it opens the floodgates to sentimentalism. Thus, despite the expansion of academic activity and teaching in the last twenty-five years, despite again the reorientation of the mainstream of African studies from its old anthropological vein towards a more avowedly historical one, there persists the notion of an essentially unchanging, a supposedly 'traditional' African past, the details of which need little researching since they can readily be assumed. While rarely spelt out explicitly, this notion flourishes as an undercurrent of contradiction in much modern historical writing and debate.

Some time back this very line of thinking was employed in the more intellectually stubborn of colonial and missionary quarters to illustrate the perpetual darkness and hopelessness of the continent unless it be saved through conversion, conquest and foreign rule. More commonly nowadays it helps conjure up an opposite picture, one which envisages an ideal Africa before it suffered interference by slave-trading and international capitalism, by Christian missionaries and foreign conquerors. Such an image of the past – if we may caricature mildly – leads to an assumption of a stable social system and economic organization in old Africa as well as permanent ecological equilibrium. This is antiquarianism, a sentimental quest for the past which in fact denies history and with it an understanding of change and development and the pressures stimulating them. It fails to appreciate the success of African agricultural iron-using communities over the last thousand years and more, and the perpetual challenges they have encountered through the resultant growth of population, in other words the crisis which each generation has had to face in feeding itself and its children. As this book tries to show, the solutions have required continual adjustments, often moderate but occasionally revolutionary, to the systems of settlement, cultivation and technology in every part of East Africa century by century.

The sentimentalist and antiquarian approach to the past – if spelled out to its logical conclusion – would see 'traditional' Africa 'safe' from the rest of the world, until supposedly its integrity was rudely shattered by international factors for which it was in no way responsible. Conceptually as well as geographically this line of thinking takes comfort in limited horizons, in a 'neo-tribalism' in effect; for those who are loudest in condemning the word 'tribe' as colonial or reactionary, and who insist on such euphemisms as 'ethnic group' for the same purpose, are those who perpetuate the very concept by offering nothing new to chew on. By taking so limited a view of Africa they render it, sadly and unfairly, an irrelevant corner of the globe.

If this book has a message it is that East Africa, the interior as much as the coast, has through the last thousand years had a place – dare we suggest a role – in the history of the world. Distinctive though it has been and dynamic in its own varied ways, its past has been no more remote, no more 'traditional' or 'pure' than that of other parts of Africa, or of the countries bordering the Indian Ocean, or indeed of the rest of the Old World. We do not set out to 'prove' this but wish simply to illustrate some of the sources available and some of the history which they convey. Though diverse in type, these historical sources are there to be used and interpreted, and are as good, we submit, as those for any other part of the world.

In doing this I need to record my appreciation of numerous colleagues, students and assistants, past and present, in the old University of East Africa and its successor universities, in the British Institute, and in the museums and antiquities services of Uganda, Tanzania and Kenya; and equally of the assistance rendered by the public in the widely spaced locations where we have travelled and surveyed, recorded and excavated in order to get this part of the way. It has been, as it must continue to be, a cooperative endeavour; to all these this digest of results and commentary are dedicated.

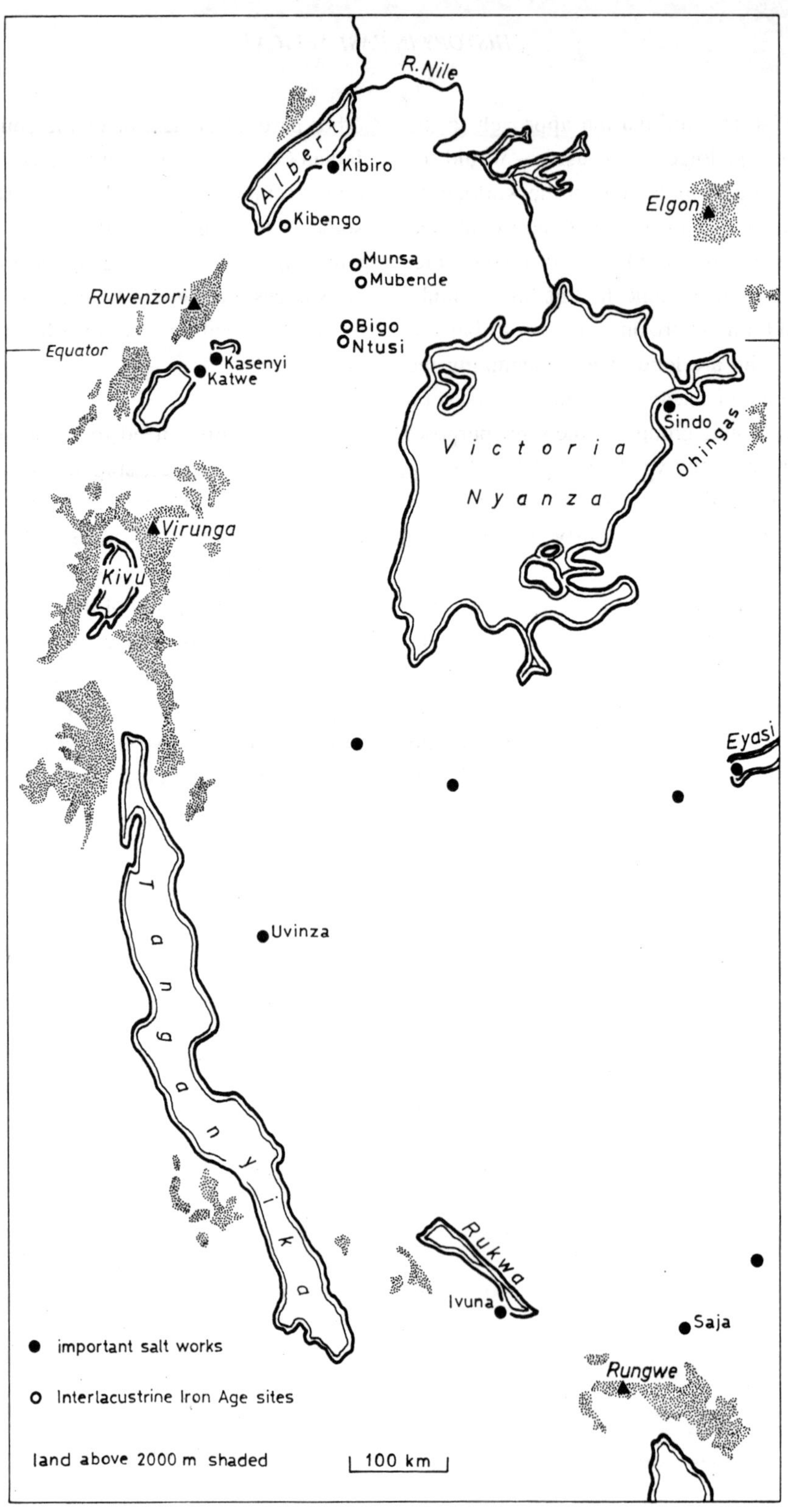
R. Nile
Albert
Kibiro
Kibengo
Elgon
Munsa
Mubende
Ruwenzori
Bigo
Ntusi
Equator
Kasenyi
Katwe
Victoria
Nyanza
Sindo
Ohingas
Virunga
Kivu
Eyasi
Uvinza
Tanganyika
Rukwa
Ivuna
Saja
Rungwe
important salt works
Interlacustrine Iron Age sites
land above 2000 m shaded
100 km

Between the Great Lakes

Those parts of East Africa bordering Lake Victoria Nyanza and towards the Western Rift Valley, enjoying good rainfall and fertile soils, have a long history of settled populations. They have thrived by the cultivation of a variety of crops, the staples in most districts being grains, principally sorghum and finger-millet. Nowadays maize, which is quite a recent introduction, supplements or actually supplants these old African cereals in many parts; but the modern success of maize has depended on adaptation of this ancient tradition of millet and sorghum cultivation. In the wetter and more heavily populated parts, however, the increasing emphasis in later centuries has been on permanent banana groves. Where rainfall is sufficient round the year, these can be more productive than grains. This varied agriculture has been balanced by specialised cattle-keeping in the fine grassland tracts.

Crops and cattle, capitals and kings

Here in western Uganda, Rwanda, Burundi and the north-westerly parts of Tanzania – often aptly called the Interlacustrine Region – cattle have carried a prestige, seemingly out of proportion to their economic importance for the rural masses. Herding has been regarded the noble pursuit. Certain ruling groups have emphasised their attachment to the pastoral life, their wealth in cattle and their distinction from the agricultural clans. This ideology has been especially developed to the west of Lake Victoria. It is impressively illustrated in Ankole and adjacent districts by the herds of humped cattle with exceptionally long horns. Appropriately, cattle and their prestige figure in the local histories and the popular legends, including those about royal heroes and the god-like personalities of antiquity known as Chwezi (or BaChwezi in plural).

The historical tradition

These historical accounts are rich and varied, ranging from mythical stories to histories of clans, and not only those of ruling ones. For commoners and rulers alike there were obvious social and political reasons for ensuring that these traditions were maintained from genera-

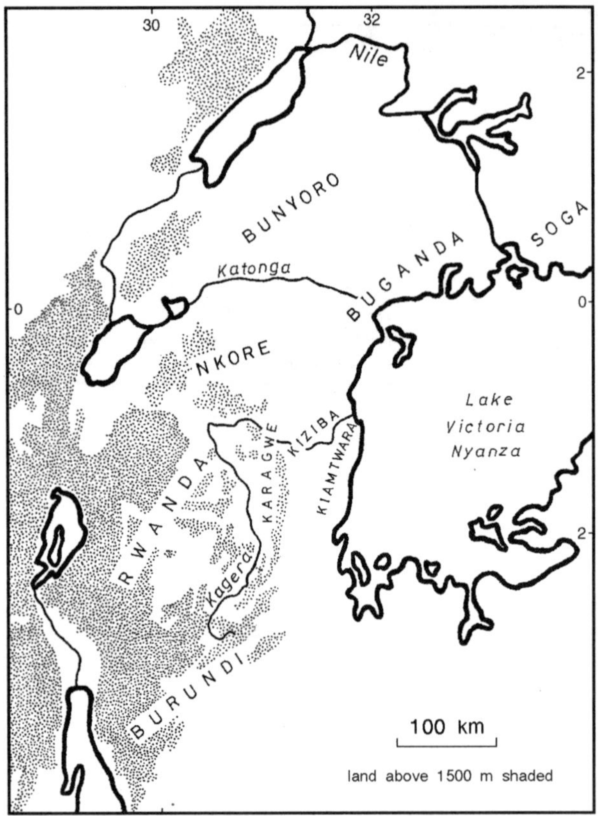

The main interlacustrine kingdoms before the 19th century

tion to generation. Often they fulfilled a religious purpose too in the form of ancestor cults.

The interpretation of the Chwezi legends remains controversial. Some hold that the (Ba)Chwezi were actual people who constituted the ruling dynasty of a powerful kingdom some five centuries ago. Remembered in some parts as Kitara, it has been considered ancestral, in direct or less direct ways, to the later kingdoms of the interlacustrine region. These are Bunyoro, Nkore (Ankole), Rwanda, Karagwe, Kiamtwara, Buganda among others, all of which thrived till very recently. But other historians would interpret this 'golden age' of the Chwezi less literally. They regard many of the stories as myths whose purpose is to explain and justify the later social and political realities of these structured kingdoms and their component clans. In this view the oral traditions remain important but require subtle interpretation through an understanding of their symbolism. For instance, certain of the legends about individual Chwezi personages are intimately connected with existing shrines, sometimes situated in groves or on hilltops; it is argued that the fame of the Chwezi spirits has been enhanced in later times by the popularity and healing powers of these religious cults and of their priests and priestesses. This in itself is of both cultural and historical significance.

These contrasting reactions to the Chwezi as recorded in interlacustrine legend (especially that of Bunyoro and Ankole) can be illustrated by excerpts from two studies published in the *Uganda Journal* (volume 22) for 1958:

> These Bacwezi were not like other men but were gods, for although they were born of women they had unending life and knew neither sickness nor death. During their reign on earth these Bacwezi conquered and ruled the countries of Ankole, Toro, Bunyoro, Buganda, Karagwe, Kiziba, Busoga and Bukedi. They eventually decided to leave the kingdom of the world because they thought it had been defiled. This is how it came about.
>
> The Bacwezi owned many cattle while on earth. Among their cattle was a cow named Bihogo bya Mpuga, which was of rare value and was regarded by the Bacwezi as the most beautiful of all their cows. One of the Bacwezi, king Wamara's nephew named Mugenyi, loved this cow so much that on one occasion he swore that whatever evil afflicted it should afflict him also; if

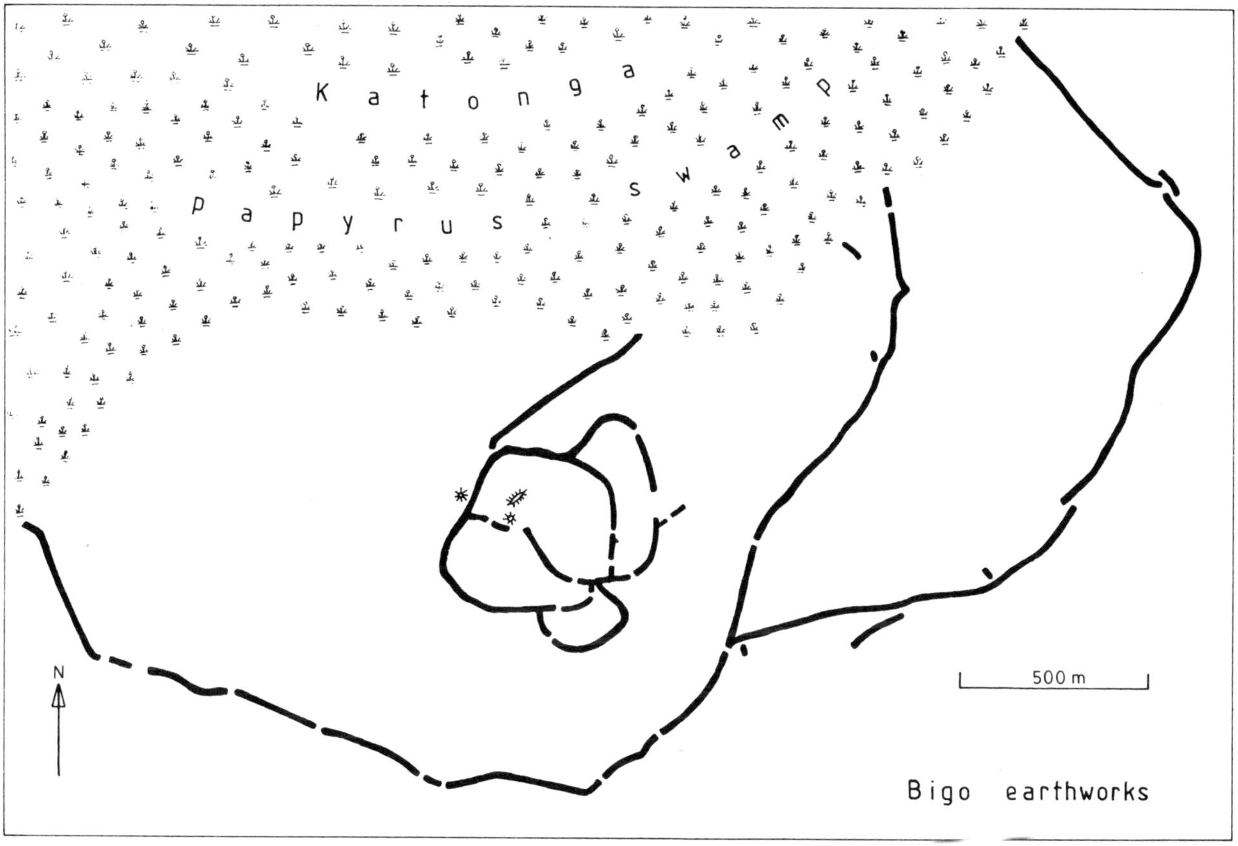

Katonga swamp
Papyrus
N
500 m
Bigo earthworks

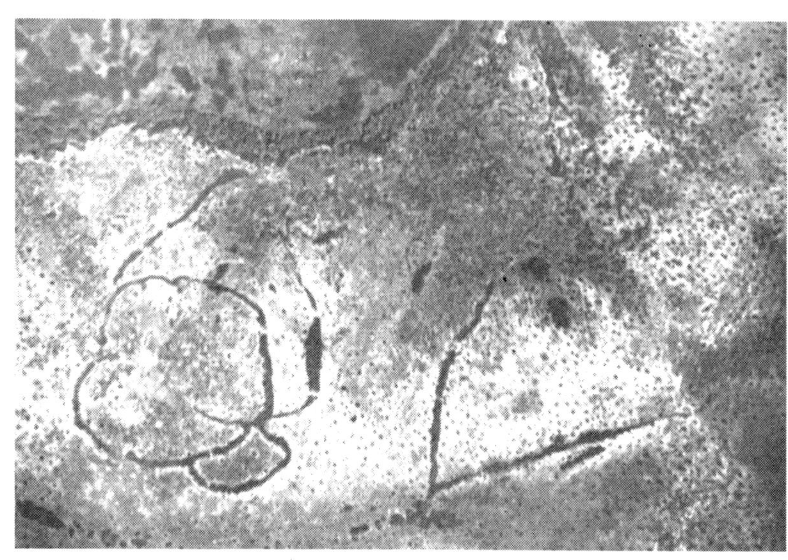

The accuracy of the plan of the Bigo earthworks drawn by Combe of the Uganda Geological Survey in 1921 is demonstrated by the air-photo, in which the ditches with their dense vegetation show up so well. Only on clearing the bushes does the form and depth of the ditches begin to come clear (as Posnansky's photograph left shows). Excavation has revealed that before silting the ditches were twice this depth. They would have been accompanied by banks of the upcast material. The central area on slightly raised ground, with its complex of ditched and banked enclosures, was an important settlement site. But its detailed purpose is not yet fully understood.

water was the cause of its death, he would never again drink a drop; if salt was the cause, none of the cattle should ever again taste salt; if it should die naturally, he would on that day kill himself.

One day when Mugenyi was sitting in the house with his friends, a boy came running and breathlessly announced that Bihogo had been seized with a fit and was at the point of death. Without a moment's hesitation Mugenyi gripped his spear to kill himself, but his brothers restrained him by force. They sought to dissuade him from his purpose by offering gifts of other cows. Although everyone sympathized with Mugenyi he was inconsolable ...

Z.C.K. Mungonya (p.19).

Compare C.C. Wrigley (p.16):

The reign of Bacwezi does not belong to the fourteenth or any other century but to the morning of the world, when the gods walked the earth. In these latter days you will not see Mugenyi driving his red cattle to the saltings, or come upon Mugasa fishing in the lake. For these *are* (and always have been) the latter days, and the gods have departed long ago, and their power can now be invoked only by a privileged few – that is to say by the human Bacwezi, the members of the priestly clans or corporations.

The supernatural attributes of the Bacwezi are not secondary (as supposed by certain historians who believe that they had existed as actual persons and rulers) but are on the contrary original and inherent. They are the lakes and the hills of south-western Uganda, the features and forces of the natural world, unusually sharply personified, and converted into kings and princes in the image of a later monarchical society.

Ancient capitals

Whatever the verdict on the Chwezi, there is certainly a long tradition of centralised government in this northern Bantu borderland. There also exist on the ground clear signs of large-scale organization between five and eight centuries ago. The best examples, in the forms of densely populated centres and great earthwork enclosures, are in western Uganda. Of the latter, the most famous is Bigo, 'the defended place', constructed against the swamps of the Katonga river in the Bwera grasslands. Here the overall length of ditches, some of which are dug five metres into the rock, exceeds ten kilometres. At their greatest extent, the Bigo ditches and ramparts enclosed some three-hundred hectares. Even before the addition of the big eastern enclosure, it would have accommodated large numbers of cattle if only for short periods – as would the rather similar earthworks at Munsa and Kibengo. Some say that Bigo was the centre where Mugenyi of Chwezi fame kept his herds; and others have gone further to imagine the central enclosure with its mounds, and the signs of occupation revealed by excavations there, as representing a royal capital of six or more centuries ago.

At the Munsa earthworks, a hundred kilometres to the north of Bigo, such banks do survive, albeit now worn down to a rounded profile.

The idea is reasonable, yet it is difficult to be certain of Bigo's purpose, which may indeed have altered over time along with the surrounding circumstances. The place was not necessarily maintained and manned permanently as a fortress. Nevertheless, the massive ditches and earthworks were obviously intended for protection – or were constructed, as is so often the case, in reaction to some dev-

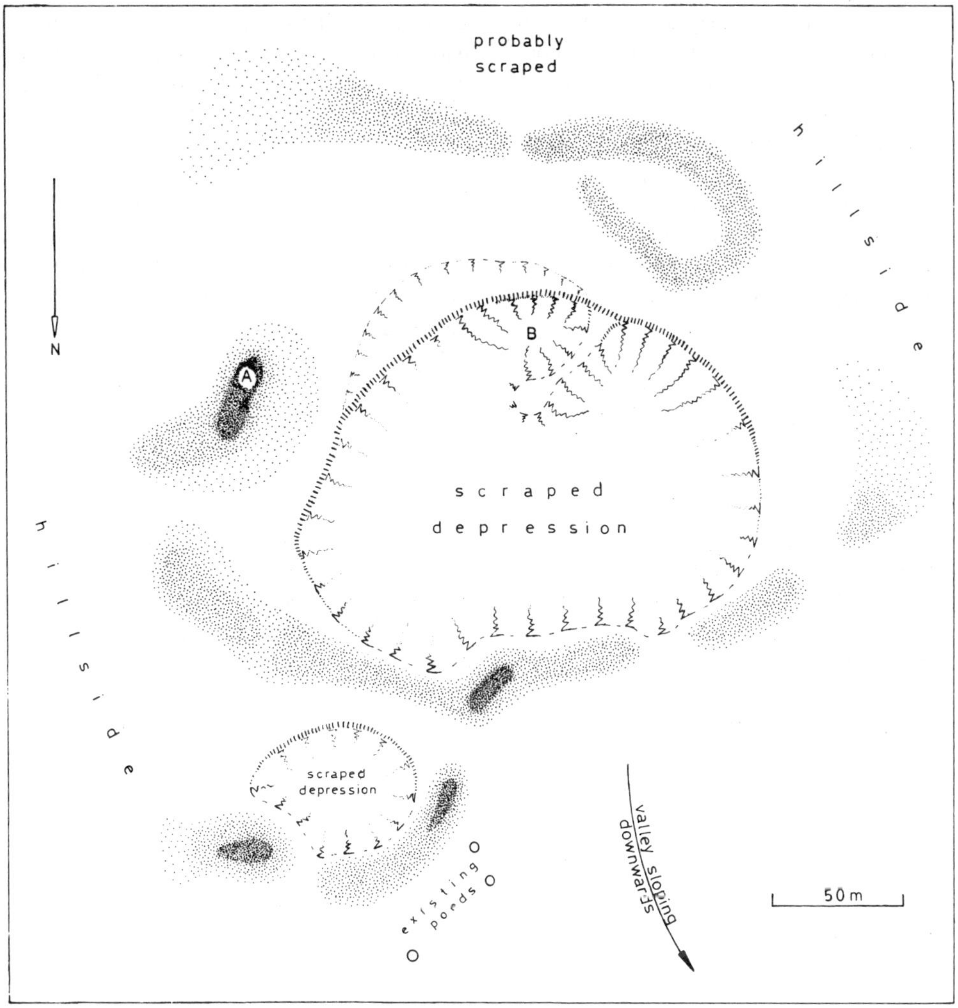

Bwogero, meaning 'the basins', at Ntusi are the result of scraping a valley bottom to the water-table. The upcast was piled in mounds (shaded on the plan) all around the basins. The top of the highest mound (A) stands 20 metres above the depression at (B). The purpose of the loop-shaped mound at the south-west remains a mystery. The photograph (Andrew Reid) shows the gap at the south, up-valley end.

astating experience, say a particularly severe bout of raiding and loss of cattle. The extensions indicate a continuing problem or periodic stresses. Whatever the exact nature and sequence of events, Bigo definitely appears to have been a centre or refuge to which the rich cattle-owners of Bwera, under their ruler perhaps, could retreat with their herds in times of insecurity. The scale of the works attests equally to their control of a body of labour with a supply of iron hoes, for both the construction and the maintenance of the great ditches and ramparts. These were conscripted presumably through the patronage which the ownership of the cattle conveyed; hence again the importance of guarding this particular source of wealth and subsistence.

The town of Ntusi

Different in form, but definitely related to the same system, was the settlement of Ntusi in the rolling grasslands overlooking Bigo. Here there are no ditched enclosures or obvious defences but signs of an important centre of population nevertheless, together with scooped-out reservoirs to provide water for cattle in an adjacent valley. Vast amounts of cattle bones litter the surface of a large area around. But the numerous inhabitants of Ntusi could not all have lived a pastoral life; for while there is a lot of grass in the district, there is not enough of it so close at hand. They relied more on their agricultural produce, for there are equally large numbers of broken pots, as well as grindstones for sorghum, all over the surface. Many hundreds if not several thousands of people must have lived here for some time. Ntusi may or may not have been a royal capital. But it certainly appears to have been a town and for that reason alone would have been politically important. The great heaps on which the inhabitants formally dumped and burnt their rubbish are an indication of the necessary civic and sanitary organization quarter by quarter.

Essential for such a population – to provide tools for domestic purposes and cultivation, as well as spears for protecting the herds – would have been a ready supply of iron. Some of this was produced on the edges of the town where remains of a smelting industry can be seen on the ground. It may have been the combined presence of rich iron-ore and fertile soil in the midst of these grasslands which recommended Ntusi for settlement in the first place. Here then are all the ingredients required for the construction and maintenance of the Bigo works only a few hours away – whether for the cultivator and labourer carrying his hoe or for the cowman walking his herd.

Excavations in the late 1980s in several of the Ntusi mounds, followed up by radiocarbon tests on carefully

Ntusi 'female' mound: apparently a refuse tip for a quarter of this town about the 11th to 13th centuries.

selected samples from different levels, reveal that the date of the settlement ranges from the 11th to the 16th centuries AD, with the concentration about the 12th and 13th centuries. We do not know the real name of this town, for it was abandoned a few hundred years ago. Later herdsmen in the district, recognising a place of ancient activity but ignorant of its history, called it simply Ntusi, meaning 'the mounds'.

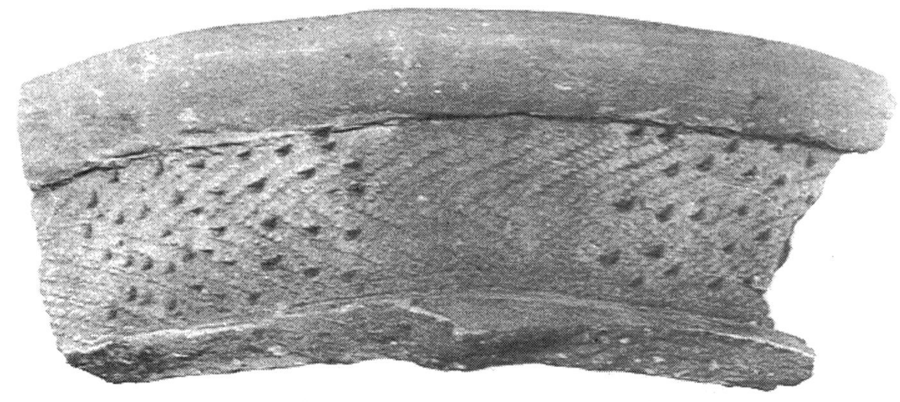

Potsherds from Ntusi (above) and Mubende

The Nyakaima tree at Mubende – popularly called the 'witch-tree' – stands some 40 metres high on this hilltop, and could be over 400 years old. It belongs to a species of Pterygota *which is known, in Lunyoro and Luganda respectively, as* ndaula/ndahura, *significantly the name of the senior Chwezi. He is at the same time the god of smallpox; and the shrine around the tree's foot (or rather between its 'toes', the long buttress roots) is connected with his wife, Nyakaima. Through her priestesses or mediums – a succession of which has attended the shrine to the present century – it possesses celebrated healing powers for a variety of illnesses, both physical and mental. Prayers, small offerings and sacrifices of white chicken continue to be made at this tree.*

Nyoro royal grave, with ceremonial spears displayed

Kings, spirits and shrines

Ntusi, with Bigo earthworks nearby and numerous lesser settlements of the period which have been located by diligent archaeological search in the intervening district, lends credence to the idea of an important polity centred in Bwera about 700 to 900 years ago, that is before the rise of the later kingdoms. It may have been part of a broader and looser confederation, to north as well as south of the Katonga swamps. Support for this view comes from Mubende Hill, which stands in the direction of the Munsa earthworks and the traditional Kitara heartland. Some six centuries ago there was a modest settlement atop this prominent hill with a cultural relationship to Bigo and Ntusi. In particular, the pottery used at all three settlements was very similar, with distinctive shapes and decorations, executed with twisted and knotted grass or string roulettes, as well as red burnishes and sometimes 'painted' designs.

As a hill, Mubende is not exceptionally high. But it rises sharply enough to afford a prospect, on the clearest of days, of the glaciers of Ruwenzori far to the west as well as Lakes Albert and Victoria in opposite directions. In a sense then one can envisage it as the very hub of the interlacustrine zone, commanding the quintessential Kitara of ancient legend. In the words of John Nyakatura, the historian of Bunyoro, as soon as King Ndahura had established Chwezi rule over Kitara he moved his capital to Mubende Hill 'so as to have a clear view of his kingdom.' (*Abakama ba Bunyoro-Kitara*, part 2, ch.2.)

The sceptics may treat that as allegorical, or wish to dismiss it as Bunyoro historical manipulation, as all part of a desire to argue a legitimate descent from legendary Kitara to later Bunyoro specifically. Nevertheless, Ndahura himself is very much present at Mubende to this day, and people frequently climb the hill to pay their respects and to consult the spirit of his wife Nyakaima. The 'witch-tree', with its towering trunk and boughs spreading majestically over the archaeological site, preserves Ndahura's name and constitutes one of the more famous shrines of the region.

If over the centuries some sites were deserted or persisted only as shrines, others, temporary and more permanent, were established. Royal abodes, which might shift from reign to reign or even within reigns, are remembered in most of the later kingdoms. Though not necessarily great centres of population – government from a royal cattle-kraal for instance would tend to be centrifugal – they provide historians with the obvious tool around which to construct the order of events and main developments. In some kingdoms the graves and jawbone reliquaries of the successive kings provide the basic chronology, and the shrines attached to them have been the conservatories of historical knowledge.

Regional history

The traditions of many of the clans, and not only the ruling ones, reveal old connections from Uganda, Rwanda and Burundi into wide parts of eastern Zaire and western Tanzania, and also right around Lake Victoria. The large stone-built enclosures called *ohinga* in South Nyanza district of Kenya – where Bantu and Lwo traditions have been merging – may be distantly related to the broader interlacustrine complex. Some of these have been built, expanded and occupied as large homesteads and cattle-enclosures in recent times.

Merging of Nilotic-speaking Lwo with Bantu has not been confined to this one district. It has occurred over several centuries through a large part of Uganda, for the Lwo peoples in the broad sense are spread out all the way from the eastern shores of Lake Victoria to the bends of the White Nile far to the north in the Sudan. The interlacustrine kingdoms constituting the northern limit of Bantu speech have been constantly exposed to this Lwo presence, and elements of the latter have been assimilated into them. It has been generally held that some of the ruling dynasties of the post-Chwezi period, notably those known as Bito which ruled in Bunyoro and Kiziba for several centuries down to the mid-twentieth, descend from Lwo conquerors.

The extent of this Lwo element has, however, been hotly disputed in some recent scholarship. But echoes may be found in parts of this zone of an ancient fear or prejudice against the very dark, heavily built and strongly armed Lwo warriors of the north, if not also against the partly Lwoized state of Bunyoro. This view, reflecting notions of the virtues of ordered settlement and established government in the old kingdoms lying south of the linguistic frontier, has perhaps been reworked in this century through a variety of external as well as internal influences.

Cattle and their history

Such narrow debate easily turns barren. More important is it to discover the factors, whether externally stimulated or not, in the development of the region, in particular the changing methods of food-production and of cattle management in view of the social and political significance of the latter. In the highlands to the east of Lake Victoria – which form the subject of the next section of this book – marked changes in the use and management of livestock can be discerned at different periods during the last eight-hundred years. One might expect roughly parallel, though certainly not identical, economic changes to have occurred between the lakes alongside the political and dynastic developments which are recorded in the local histories.

Whereas cattle have been kept in the high grasslands close to the Rift Valley of Kenya and northern Tanzania for quite three-thousand years, in the lush pastures of the interlacustrine zone their history seems a lot shorter. If cattle were used in the earliest stages of the Iron Age – the period from about two-thousand years ago which saw the radiation of eastern Bantu cultivating peoples from this region – their importance then was rather slight. Quite plausibly it was not till around the middle of the Iron Age, 1000 AD or so, that specialised herding began here. Such a development could coincide perhaps with Lwo or earlier Nilotic pressures from the northern side. The Ntusi excavations attest large numbers of cows no later than that time.

An interesting contrast, one persisting through this thousand-year period, stands out between this interlacustrine region and the highlands to the east (including Maasailand). Though in both there has been a fair degree of dairy specialisation, in the east smaller and shorter-horned humped cattle were preferred. Moreover, small stock, both goats and sheep, have played an integral role in the pastoral economies there, both in Maasai times and long before, whereas in the interlacustrine region they have not on the whole been combined with cattle in a big way. Here goats are regarded more as the animals of the cultivators, not of the true herdsmen.

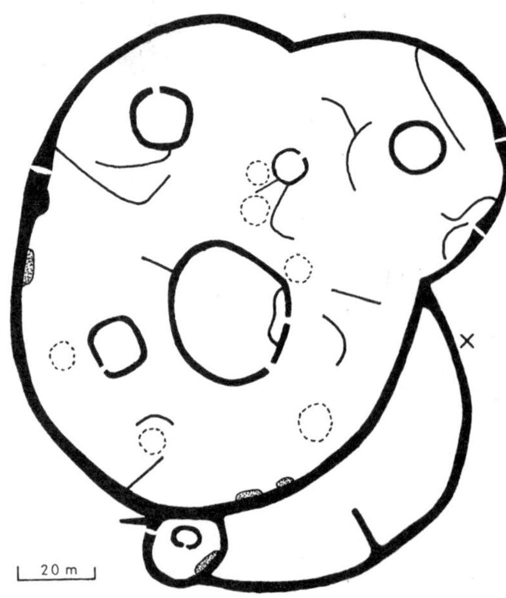

Thimlich ohinga*: sketch plan (after Laurel Phillipson in* Azania *II) of stone-walled enclosure and main internal features. The entrances into the main enclosure are all covered and lintelled (as in photograph). Some of the interior enclosures doubtless represent pens for cattle or small stock or contained houses. Several house outlines are detectable. Outside the eastern wall (at X) iron-working had been practised, as shown by a concentration of smithing waste.*

Farmers and herders

But in both regions, more specialised herding practices and the increased prestige attached to owning cattle were dependent in one way or another on substantial populations of developed cultivators. Pure pastoralism, involving not only a refusal to cultivate but in some cases a prohibition against accepting vegetable foods, can in the best of situations be pursued only by a minority. It requires the services of craftsmen, for manufacture of iron tools, pots and often leatherwork; it requires also agricultural populations round and about who can absorb the pastoral overspill which the grasslands cannot support, and in particular provide succour and relief during runs of drought years or following heavy losses through cattle disease.

By this view therefore, the 'pure' pastoral ideal is not aboriginal, but a late development, the result of polarisation within a mixed economy. The evidence from Ntusi, where large numbers of cattle were brought into an essentially agricultural community from the surrounding grasslands, may illustrate the early stages of such polarisation in the western Ugandan grasslands nine to seven centuries ago. As this process went further, decentralization became necessary, so that Ntusi and the earthwork sites including Bigo had to be abandoned. There may be other explanations for Ntusi, for both its success and its eventual decline; further research will tell. But in any case it was unlike settlements of more recent times, which shows that big changes occurred in the region around the 15th or 16th century.

If then Ntusi and Bigo are ancestral to the later kingdoms of this region, it is in a general sense only. These places should not be claimed as belonging to any particular kingdom of recent memory. They lie in the buffer zone, or nomansland, between Nkore, Bunyoro and Buganda, none of which ever had its centre in the Bwera parklands or the Katonga swamps. Here largely independent clans or adventurous elements seceding from one kingdom or another maintained their frontier fiefdoms and enjoyed the local wealth and power which the grasslands and their cattle generated.

Rulers and ruled

Now, it is commonly held that in these western interlacustrine districts the cattle-keeping minority (*Hima* in Ankole, *Tutsi* in Rwanda) has always been separate from the common cultivators (*Iru* and *Hutu*). Distinct origins have been assumed, the cattle-keepers often regarded as conquering invaders of several centuries ago. That is how John Hanning Speke, the first European to enter the region, understood the social and political situation in the 1860s. Combining his own prejudices (as a British army officer in India) with the propaganda provided by the Hinda court of Karagwe and by Nyoro and Ganda informants, he neatly summed it up with a chapter-heading 'Theory of conquest of inferior by superior races' (in *The Journal of the Discovery of the Source of the Nile* 1863). He surmised that the ruling and aristocratic minority had some time previously invaded from Ethiopia; probably, he thought, they were a branch of the Oromo (or Galla, as he called them, sections of whom he had encountered a few years previously while accompanying Richard Burton from the Gulf of Aden to the city of Harar).

While no historian nowadays would present the issue in so starkly racialist or diffusionist a way, this notion of a separate northern origin for the pastoral elites of the interlacustrine region has persisted. And these elites have had of course an interest in perpetuating it. Yet persuasive historical evidence to support this line is difficult to find, and the linguistic situation argues strongly against it. The Hima and Tutsi minorities share the Bantu language of the Iru and Hutu cultivators, and no-one has detected traces of a Cushitic substratum in the region related to Oromo or any other Ethiopian tongue.

Social and economic changes

That the social, cultural and economic divisions are and have been real is undeniable. There are also physical differences, in height and facial features. But some popular descriptions exaggerate. The tall pastoralists are *not* necessarily lighter-skinned than members of the agricultural clans; frequent statements that they are of 'north African' type or even 'European-looking' are quite erroneous. The differences may have nothing to do with origins; more likely they result from the same cultural separation and contrasting diets coupled with in-breeding within the pastoral minority. This process should stretch back to the period when cattle-keeping was first sufficiently established to provide exchangeable wealth and the prestige and patronage which went with it, and the agricultural base was at the same time adequately developed to support through thick and thin this form of distinct but dependent specialisation.

Of course, the royal and clan traditions contain little hint of such social and economic change. As internal sources they are important, but at the same time they ought to invite modern historians to reexamine and reinterpret in the light of other evidence. Moreover, the heroic element in these traditions, reaching back twenty or more generations to the supposed founders of the pastoral dynasties in the western grasslands, if not beyond them to the Chwezi of ancient Kitara, has caused them to be further romanticized in later telling. As a result important but more mundane developments in the region have been concealed somewhat.

By the 18th century the power bases of the pastoral rulers were being eclipsed by those controlling thicker populations in the highlands to their west as well as those along the north-western shores of Lake Victoria. Here in Buganda the expansion of banana cultivation at the expense of sorghum went hand-in-hand with spectacular demographic increase; and while the kings maintained much of the old regional pastoral ideology, in practice they and their administrative elite liberated themselves from it. Thus they reaped military, economic and political success, the fruits of which have persisted till the present century. A hundred years ago the Swahili form of the name Buganda, that is Uganda, was adopted by the British for a much bigger chunk of Africa, one in which however Buganda remained influential and central in more than a simply geographical sense.

Production and Trade

The various agricultural and pastoral specialisations within these interlacustrine communities encouraged interaction and exchange through markets at regular or seasonal intervals. Certain products – basketry, pots, barkcloth and leatherwork for instance – required expert craftsmen and women who passed on the skills to their children or apprentices. More specialised and local were iron-working and salt-production, both dependent on suitable mineral resources. This was especially true of fine salt, whose places of production could become important markets for the longer-distance trade. (See map on p.4.)

Salt industries and markets

Among agricultural communities salt is always in demand. It is obtainable in many ways. These include burning of particular grasses and diluting of saline soils in certain low-lying areas and lakesides, followed by filtering and boiling. Such laborious techniques are frequently encountered. But rich sources of fine salt, prepared from brine-wells or saline lakes or from the vicinity of hot springs in volcanic regions, are rare inland and became therefore centres of industry and exchange. Salt, by the bundle or basket, was often a standard against which other commodities were measured. Along the trade routes its value increased with distance. This is well documented in the interlacustrine region and further afield in Zaire and Tanzania.

Excavations at Ivuna, Uvinza and Kibiro saltworks have revealed long industrial histories. Uvinza in particular has an unlimited supply of excellent brine, whose processing into fine salt dictated the routes of the caravans. Here the brine was so pure that normally it required no filtering. The industry was described in 19th-century travel literature. The excavations there have discovered much more, a sequence of some fifteen centuries of activity.

At Kibiro and Ivuna the industrial sequences seem not so long, less than a thousand years yet definitely more than five-hundred in each case. The salt lakes at Kasenyi and Katwe in the Western Rift are known from local records to have been exploited since the 18th century at least. Presumably the different types of salt available there were used and traded long before; but this remains to be verified by proper archaeological investigations of those places.

Uvinza in the 19th century

The Uvinza saltworks, sometimes inaccurately called 'pans', consist of a number of springs of pure and concentrated brine which rise through weak points in the underlying rock around the confluence of the Malagarasi and Ruchugi rivers.

The 19th-century situation, with regular long-distance caravans carrying and seeking merchandise in several directions and connecting through the coast with international commerce, was different in scale from that of earlier centuries. But it is worth reproducing here the first-hand observations of Uvinza by travellers of the 1850s to

Salt and cooking soda are commonly prepared at source by diluting salty soil with water and filtering through a large pot with a hole in its base closed by tough stalks; the solution seeps through this filter leaving the sand in the pot (as here at Saja on the Sangu plains in southern Tanzania).

The process may need repeating twice or thrice until sufficient purity is obtained. The brine is then boiled in another pot (or a metal container these days) over a wood fire. As the water evaporates, a residue of salt – grey or brown or white – is left.

Soda for cooking or softening hard or desiccated vegetables is produced in similar ways. Often one gets mixtures of common salt (sodium chloride) and soda (sodium carbonate and/or bicarbonate – with obvious medicinal properties), as well as small proportions of other salts.

The lower photograph shows such soda preparation at Ikoga, also on the Sangu plains. In this case the process begins not with collected soil, but with a hardy grass which grows on slightly salty soils and stores the salt in its stalks. These are burnt and the ashes diluted, for filtering and boiling in the same way. This plant, Zaleya pentandra, *is recorded as being used for a similar purpose across a large part of the African savannas, as far west as Timbuktu.*

1870s. Their accounts are brief; moreover, none stopped long enough to witness and understand the whole business. But with the assistance of oral memories, of records of the German period (around 1900) and of archaeological investigations in 1967, a picture has been obtained of the former salt-working activity and of the situation within which this industry and trade were pursued.

The explorer Richard Burton, who passed through Uvinza twice in 1858, left the first written account of the place, commenting on the quality of the salt, which being

> far superior to the bitter, nitrous produce of Ugogo, finds its way throughout the heart of Africa, supplying the lands adjoining both the Tanganyika and the Nyanza Lakes.

Excavations by the Pwaga brine-spring at Uvinza produced evidence of salt-working from the Early Iron Age down to the 19th century. In the later period clay tanks were constructed for storage or partial evaporation of the brine, before it was boiled in large earthenware pots supported on hearth stones over wood fires. These tanks, as seen, were cut into earlier levels of hearths and wood-ash.

In the present century the basic techniques are unchanged, but the scale, detail and organization are different, as shown by the solar evaporation pans.

By the Pwaga brine-spring he found

> a settlement of Wavinza, containing from forty to fifty bee-hive huts, tenanted by salt-diggers. The principal pan is sunk in the vicinity of the river, the saline produce, after being boiled down in the huts, is piled up, and handmade into little cones. The pan affords tripartite revenue to three sultans, and it constitutes the principal wealth of the Wavinza. (*The Lake Regions of Central Africa*, II, p.37.)

Commander V.L. Cameron, travelling the same route in 1874 (in search of David Livingstone supposedly), was equally impressed:

> A very good white salt, the best of any I have seen in Africa. This salt is carried far and wide. The whole district from Lake Victoria Nyanza, round the south of Lake Tanganyika, much of Manyema, and south to the Ruaha, is supplied by the pans of Uvinza.
>
> There are some other places in these districts where salt is produced, but that of Uvinza is so superior that it always finds a ready sale. (*Across Africa*, I, p.232.)

The brine-springs (marked by black dots) around the Ruchugi-Malagarasi confluence at Uvinza (after E. G. Haldemann). The railway from Dar es Salaam through Tabora to Lake Tanganyika and the 'little north' road both date from early in the twentieth century.

But it was not the time of year for activity:

> On both banks of the Rusugi (*sic*) there were temporary villages now quite deserted, innumerable broken pots, stone fire-places, and small pits where people make salt in the season (p.234).

A similar situation was found by Henry M. Stanley, fording the Ruchugi at the same point two years later:

> Near the crossing on either side are the salt-pans of Uvinza, which furnish a respectable revenue to its king. A square mile of ground is strewn with broken pots, embers of fires, the refuse of the salt, lumps of burnt clay, and ruined huts. (*Through the Dark Continent*, p.325.)

In the season this place clearly served as both factory and market.

Production and profit

Stanley alluded to the tax levied on the salt produced and sold. Two decades earlier Burton had observed a more complex arrangement, whereby *three* Vinza 'sultans' (or chiefs) each exacted a 'tripartite revenue'. The territorial boundaries of the chiefdoms all met at the concentration of brine springs around the Malagarasi-Ruchugi confluence. From other records, including local memories, it appears that each ruler took his turn, one year in three, to collect the tax. That at least was the theoretical arrangement; in practice there were frequent and bitter disputes over the control of this exceptional economic resource. Thus, between Burton's visit and that of Stanley, one chief, Ruzunzu by name, managed to defeat or overawe the others and monopolise the whole production. The salt could be exchanged for food, cloth and a range of other traded goods, not the least of them being arms and ammunition.

Uvinza's salt was worked in the dry season, not only because that was the time when labour was freed from cultivation, but also because during rains with the rivers in flood the brine in the springs became too dilute. Each year after the harvest the springs were re-opened ceremonially by a priest or ritual expert. As the salt-season approached, people flocked from near and far. In the hills of the Burundi border, it was regarded as part of a young man's coming-of-age to join the annual Uvinza safari and to return home with his load of salt. The industry absorbed a lot of labour, not just for boiling the brine but equally for cutting firewood as well as for porterage and all sorts of ancillary services. The evaporation process was dependent on mass-production of coarse open-mouthed pots. They were treated roughly in this industrial situation: hence the piles and broad scatter of broken vessels which were noted by the 19th-century travellers and which remain obvious to this day by the old springs.

The importance of Uvinza and its salt has persisted through the 20th century. In 1902 the industry was taken over by a German company, which was granted a monopoly by the new government and which technically compensated the Vinza chiefs. Most of the brine springs were closed in time, while two were adapted for a more mechanized industry with deeper bore-holes and pumps and bigger evaporation devices (both boilers and solar pans). The central railway has provided the transport of the product throughout Tanzania and also into countries beyond (the Lake Tanganyika steamers carrying it to what are now Zambia, Zaire and Burundi). The story of Uvinza is thus one of industrial continuity in which increasing and more distant demands have been answered by enlargement of scale through periodic technical innovations.

Technology

Iron and agriculture

While salt has been necessary for the health and cuisine of the cultivating communities, iron has become an increasingly essential commodity for efficient clearance of the land, tending of the fields and reaping of the crops, as well as for all sorts of domestic purposes.

The Iron Age of eastern Africa is in fact about two-thousand years old. (Reliance on cutting tools of stone was superseded so long ago that no memory of the Stone Age remains.) Some of the best available evidence of early iron-working and iron-using has come to light in the western lacustrine region, notably Rwanda and north-western Tanzania.

From that time iron has been central to African technology, culture and economy, and thus for feeding the increasing populations. The frequent symbolic importance of the iron hoe derives from this economic reality.

Iron and government

Control of the supplies of iron has meant therefore wealth and power. For, though iron is a common mineral, rich sources of workable ore are less frequent, and the skills of producing usable metal from it are complex. This extraction from dull clays and sands is in effect a magic, which particular families and guilds would keep secret. In some areas the two main stages of the process – *smelting* (NOT melting) of the ore in the furnace, and afterwards *smithing* of actual tools in the forge – have been the preserve of different specialists.

Just as the hoe may signify the agricultural prosperity of the people, or again as the smith's hammer signifies strength and skill, so the iron spear has signified power and command in an equally obvious way. The intimate connection between iron and government is a frequent theme, in the interlacustrine region and several parts of Tanzania for instance. But how often kings literally fed the charcoal fire and wielded the hammer depends on how one likes to interpret historical records.

Struggles for power

This theme is nicely illustrated in the history of the Usambara mountains in eastern Tanzania (extending somewhat the geographical range of this section). Before Mbega – supposedly the founder of the Kilindi royal line – could consolidate his government some two centuries ago, he had to overawe one Tuli, the leader of the black-smithing clan who commanded popular support. Mbega succeeded through his charisma and superior magic. There are several versions of the story told in the language of Usambara, one of which was turned into Swahili for permanent record in the 1890s by Abdallah bin Hemedi.

> Na yule mzee Tuli akapigiwa vigelegele, akajisifu ufundi wa kufua, akajisifu usemi, akajisifu moto, akajisifu kuua Wapare kwa mkuki wake, akajisifu kufua mishale, na miundu, na mashoka, na visu, na mikuki, na kujua kufanya vikuku, akajisifu kuwa tajiri wa ng'ombe, na mbuzi, na kondoo, akajisifu kutunza watu wote, na kuwahurumia; Kila ajisifulo huwauliza watu wake, Maneno haya nisemayo ni uwongo ao kweli. Wale watu wake humwitikia husema kwa pamoja, Ni kweli.

> Tuli their headman was received with loud shouts of applause, and he proclaimed his skill in metal work, and his eloquence, and glorified the fire of his forge, and boasted how he slew the men of Pare with his spear, and how he beat out arrows and swords and axes and knives and spears, and he could make bracelets, and he boasted that he was rich in cattle and goats and sheep, and he proclaimed that it was he who protected all the people

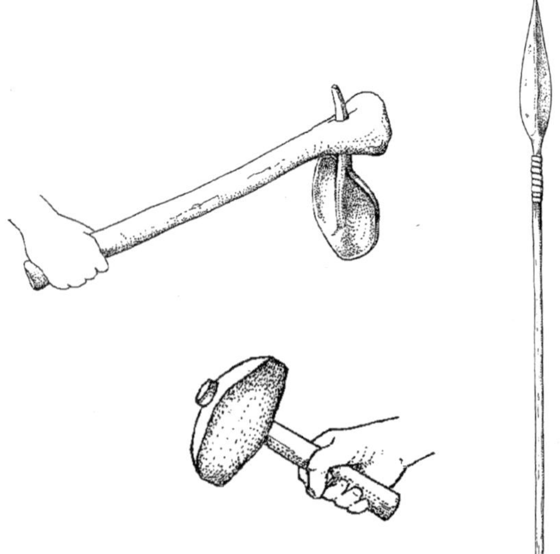

and cared for them with gentle kindness; and at every word he asked his people, 'Is this that I say true or false?' And his people responded with one voice, 'It is true.'

Habari za Wakilindi by Abdallah bin Hemedi'lAjjemy was republished in 1962 by the East African Literature Bureau, and the English edition (*The Kilindi*) in 1963, edited by J.W.T. Allen (a Swahili scholar) and William Kimweri Mbago (of the Kilindi clan). The passages quoted are from chapter XI. The translation is essentially that of Roland Allen in *Tanganyika Notes and Records* 2 (1936), p. 83. Though a competent rendering, it may not capture fully the strident rhythm of the Swahili in recounting the confrontation between the rival leaders.

Abdallah bin Hemedi, who recorded this version of the legend, was not native to Usambara: as a youth he had run away from Zanzibar where he had received an upper-class education. With this advantage he became a prominent official at the court of the last independent rulers of the Kilindi house. His version of events cannot be considered impartial therefore. (But Tuli gets a full and fair treatment, perhaps because Abdallah took a wife of that clan.) The story enshrines the legitimacy of the winning party, the Kilindi succession claiming descent from Mbega. But whether Mbega himself actually existed – he is remembered as a skilful hunter as well as a magician, and his name should mean the hairy colobus monkey of the forest – has been doubted by some recent historians. Real person or heroic personification, what matters is the historical role Mbega has played in the minds of later generations and the explanation of the foundation of Kilindi government over this fertile massif. This kingly clan was specifically not an iron-working one; yet it had to control, through special powers and effective political leadership, the supply of hoes and axes, of spears and arrows throughout its realm.

Among these powers, essential to the health of the kingdom and to the survival of each king in succession, was rain-making. For, though the Usambara hills are naturally fertile, the resultant density of population depends on an assured supply of bananas and an annual grain harvest too. The rains usually come; it is essential that they *always* do so.

Royal 'treasure-houses'

Ritual smithing is well documented in several of the interlacustrine kingdoms, however, and the metaphor or symbolism is sometimes extended in the telling. It was connected, in a conceptual way, to the wellbeing of the state. In Karagwe, now in the north-western corner of Tanzania, an amazing collection of over a hundred iron objects is attributed to the hand of a previous king and marvellous smith, Ndagara. No-one saw him at it of course, for he worked secretly by night (and strangely no-one was awoken by the striking of the hammer on the anvil). Among his feats was the forging of a special hammer which he hurled across the Kagera valley into Rwanda where it struck and killed his enemy, king Gahindiro. That is the Karagwean version of the episode, which is not exactly corroborated by the Rwandese historical authorities!

This Karagwe collection has been kept at the old capital of Bweranyange. It has served as a royal museum, or 'treasure-house' as Stanley described it in 1876. (It is now somewhat depleted, some specimens having been taken to museums overseas, others sadly damaged, lost or looted in this century.) The ironwork includes many non-utilitarian objects and ceremonial weapons, as well as the famous models of long-horned cows. As in all the interlacustrine kingdoms, there are also the royal drums, with their individual names and traditional significance, and other objects of wood, barkcloth and leather. Copperwork is included, as are cowrie-shells from the Indian Ocean. Together these suggest that part of the collection may date to the period of the trading caravans which connected with the coast in the 19th century.

Whatever the actual ages of the individual items, the tradition of royal collections of metalwork and of other special and ritual objects is an old one, not only here in Karagwe but also in Rwanda and adjacent parts of Uganda. Some pieces in Ankole and Bunyoro are claimed to belong to the earliest 'Chwezi' kings of five or more centuries ago. That may be difficult to prove; nevertheless the idea of antiquity and originality is important in itself. Equally perplexing is the combination of items of much older iron-working equipment deriving from the *early* Iron Age as much as two-thousand years ago. This does not imply continuity in a simple sense. Yet, together with the position of certain later shrines, associated with the names of Chwezi and Hinda kings, on several such ancient sites including those of actual

The 'treasure house, arms and treasures of Rumanika', king of Karagwe, at Bweranyange, as illustrated in H.M. Stanley, Through the Dark Continent *(London, 1878). Stanley's original notebook contains much more accurate drawings than those rendered by the publisher's artist.*

iron-smelting activities, it emphasises once again the centrality of iron and of the skills of working it in the material and spiritual life of the region.

Smelting furnaces

The length of the African Iron Age has allowed innumerable opportunities for technical experiment and improvement and for the development of regional, sometimes very local, traditions. Smelting furnaces in particular are extremely variable in shape and size, and in details of operation too. This variability may depend partly on the different types of ore. Thus the biggest furnaces are not necessarily the best or the most productive: they are designed for handling large quantities of unrefined 'bog-iron' requiring vast amounts of charcoal and a long, slow smelt. The labour of cutting suitable trees and preparing charcoal must be noted as another important factor affecting the cost and competitiveness of the finished product.

Some of the much smaller furnaces using refined magnetite ore can produce an equal amount of excellent wrought iron more efficiently and cheaply. On the other hand, the tall 'chimney' furnaces do save on labour in one part of the process since they induce their own draught, making bellows work unnecessary. But even then the product needs a lot of laborious refining on a small secondary furnace, requiring heavy hammer and

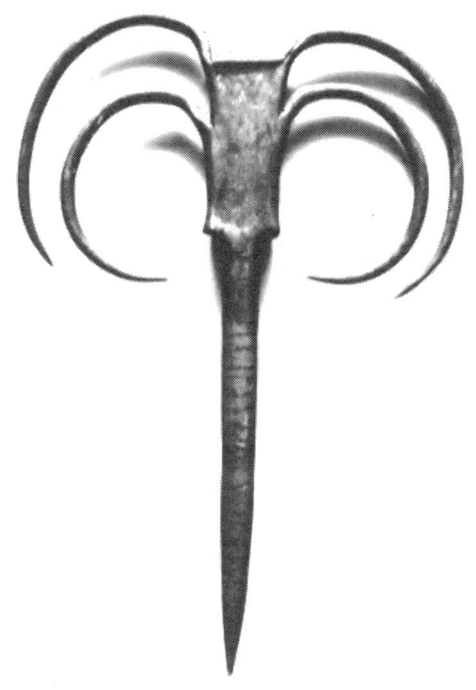

Bweranyange collection: ceremonial iron anvil measuring 67 cm (photo, Hamo Sassoon) and models of long-horned cows, 30 cm long (side and front view, illustrated by Caroline Sassoon)

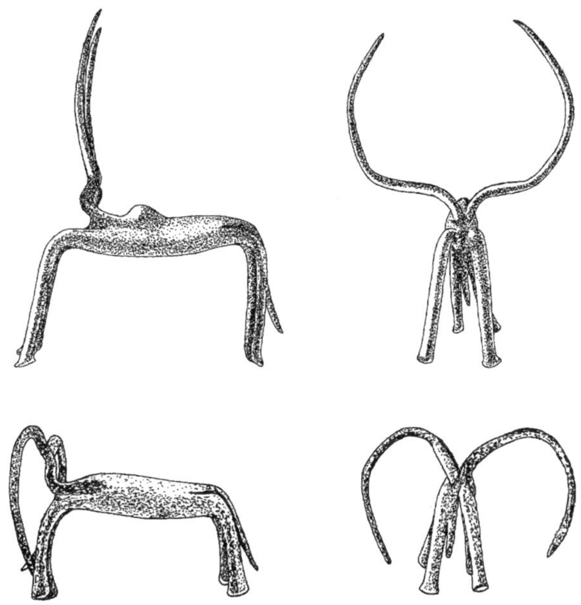

Iron anvils with prongs, called nyarushara, *forming part of the royal insignia of Rwanda (photo, R. Bourgeois)*

Iron-smelting about 1900 in Ungoni, southern Tanzania (F. Fülleborn, Das Deutsche Njassa- und Ruwuma-Gebiet *1906), and a disused small shaft furnace in Ukinga in the southern highlands. Smelting is a male profession, the furnace being regarded as female, with as here a pair of breasts modelled on the clay wall, to signify fertility or at least the hope of a productive smelt.*

Chimney furnaces which induce their own draught are frequent in the Tanganyika-Nyasa corridor, especially in Ufipa. That on the left was built and used in the 1940s, the other, with scaffolding to assist loading, was constructed for an experimental smelt at the Village Museum in Dar es Salaam in 1967. Similar furnaces were recorded in Ufipa in the late 19th century.

Remains of a recent shaftless 'bowl' furnace in northern Kenya (scale in 10 cm sections)

Ngoni forge with bowl bellows (Fülleborn); South Pare forge with bag bellows

bellows work, before being ready for fashioning into hoes. This middle part of the process is sometimes unnecessary in districts with the best magnetites which are smelted in small or medium furnaces.

Technical variety

Another possible explanation of variation in furnaces and smelting techniques may be sought in the demands placed on the industry – for instance different qualities of wrought iron and mild steel needed for fashioning different types of tools and weapons required district by district. There may be other, less practical, reasons. We need to know more about development through time in individual regions. The furnaces illustrated here are all of the last one hundred years; and though they certainly reflect long traditions, we cannot insist that there had been no changes during the preceding centuries – let alone over the whole two-thousand years of the Iron Age. Doubtless there were, as the industry had to respond to new requirements in either the quality or the quantity of its products. The industrial archaeology of East Africa remains a challenge. It is being taken up: the most revealing work so far has been in Kivu, Rwanda and north-western Tanzania.

Smithing too has its innumerable variations in detail, most conspicuously in the types of skin bellows used to supply a draught through the clay pipe (tuyere) to the charcoal fire.

Ancient and modern industry

Broken tuyeres found on the ground or in eroded exposures are a frequent sign of ancient metallurgy. If one notices also pieces of a fired clay wall or furnace base or large amounts of slag lying around, one can conclude that it was a smelting site, not a forge. The slag represents the waste material from the reduction process. Whereas the iron content of the ore separates as a spongy red-hot 'bloom' (which is afterwards removed for further treatment by hammering over heat in the forge), the more voluminous waste runs off, dropping into the base of the furnace or oozing out through the tuyeres and holes. On cooling it forms black vesicular lumps. Unlike the iron then, much of this slag actually *melts* and thus gives rise to the misunderstanding that the iron itself is melted.

Iron can be melted of course in some modern industrial processes which allow much higher temperatures to be attained. But the *cast* iron so produced is too brittle for hammering into knives, hoes or spears. For these one requires *wrought* iron or mild steel produced by *smelting* with charcoal and a good draught in the ways described, at temperatures around 1000°C or somewhat above. Local variations and periodic developments and market responses notwithstanding, these basic principles have been maintained across the middle of Africa for some two-thousand years.

During the 20th century African iron industries have gone into sharp decline in the face of imported goods and new technology. In very few places indeed is smelting now practised; in most districts the art is already lost (although museums in several countries have attempted, with different levels of success, revival experiments for purposes of filming and historical recording). Smithing however continues to flourish by refurbishing old tools, manufacturing new ones and handling all sorts of local repair needs (including bicycles and wheelbarrow fittings), by putting to use old car-springs and other such scrap. In countries facing import restrictions, the demands on scrap iron and on the skills of working it become noticeably enhanced in the small towns and the countryside.

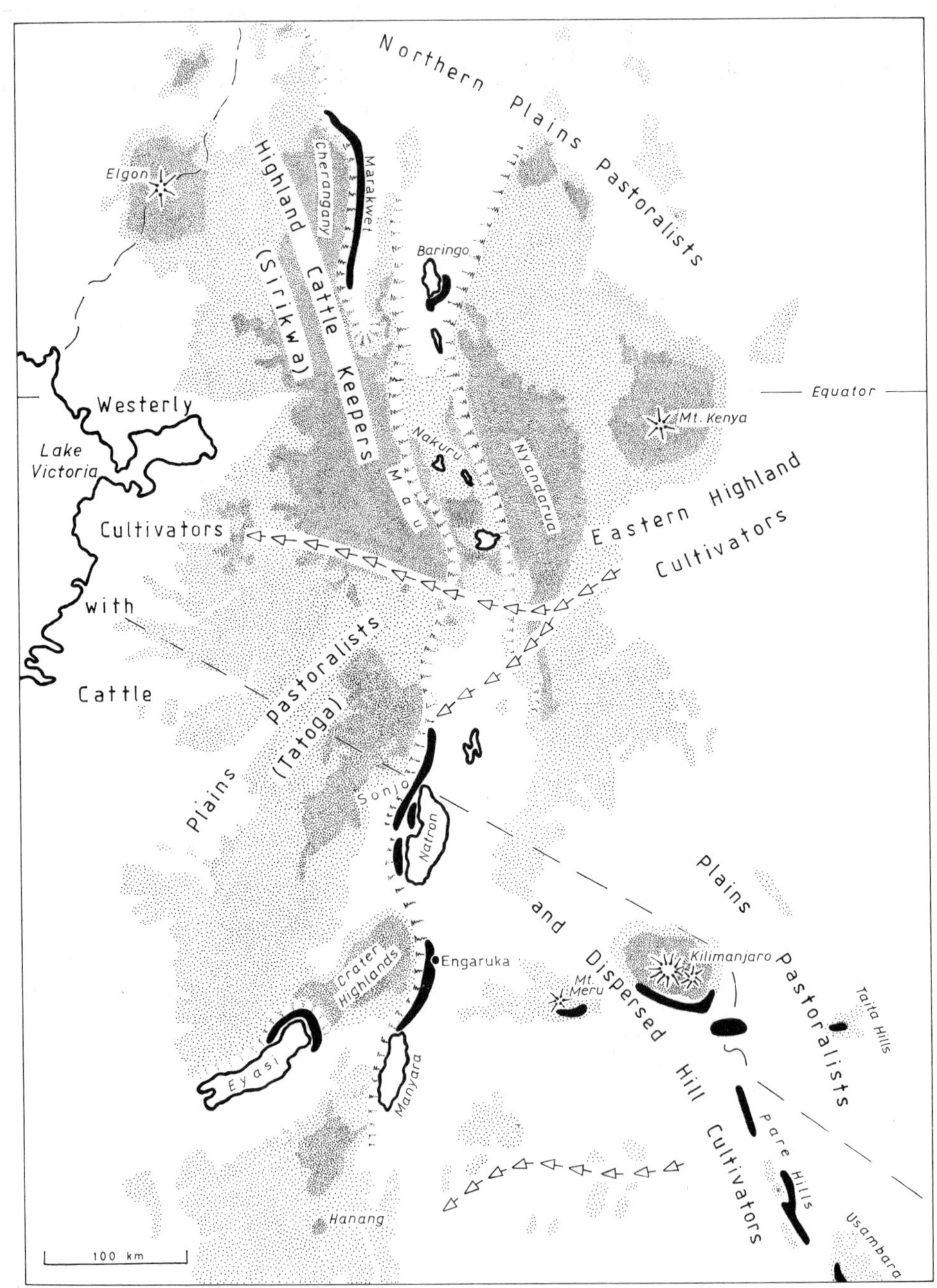

The highlands and grasslands of Kenya and northern Tanzania about 400 years ago (before the Maasai expansion). Areas of ancient irrigation agriculture shown solid. The Rift Valley, running north-south through the central highland mass, is indicated by the facing escarpments and line of lakes. The shading is at altitudes of 1500 and 2000 m.

The Rift Valley and Highlands before the Maasai

Between the Lake Regions and the Coast lies the volcanic highland zone of Kenya and northern Tanzania, bisected by the Eastern Rift Valley. The highlands are very uneven, mostly ranging in altitude between 1,500 and 3,000 metres (5,000 to 10,000 feet), with some mountains rising considerably above that. Moreover, the Rift Valley, running from north to south, is not a simple trough; the Nakuru-Naivasha stretch, often called the 'Central Rift', is elevated to almost 2,000 metres. Altogether this is a region of frequent if not sudden variation, not only in altitude but equally in rainfall and vegetation, with fine tracts of pasture frequently adjoining fertile hills or montane forest. Thus productive agriculture is and has been pursued close to successful specialised cattle-rearing, with room being left in the forests for small bands of expert hunters and honey-collectors.

The Elgeyo escarpment, with a drop of over 1200 metres from the fine plateau grasslands of Uasin Gishu and its forested fringe to the Kerio valley.

The extensive pastures of the Crater Highlands range between 2,000 and 3,000 metres in altitude.

This natural richness and variety have allowed numerous opportunities for communities to combine their specialisations or to exchange the products. With cattle, goats and sheep being kept for at least three-thousand years, and grain-cultivation possibly practised for an equal length of time, stretching back well before the Iron Age, the history of these highlands is unusually complex.

Louis Leakey and the archaeological tradition

This region has received more archaeological attention than any other in East Africa, beginning with the pioneer work of Louis Leakey in the 1920s, which concentrated on the Nakuru-Elmenteita basin in the Central Rift. Much of Leakey's research was on the various periods of the Stone Age, but a good part of it dealt with the very latest stages overlapping with pottery and food-production, what has often been called 'Neolithic'. In the early days of research the significance of Iron Age sites, relating to the history of the existing peoples, was poorly appreciated. In time, however, priorities have changed, and the importance of the Iron Age, especially its recent centuries, for understanding the present population of the region, has been increasingly acknowledged during the last thirty years. Central to this endeavour has been dating by the radiocarbon technique which, while not necessarily yielding the precise age of every archaeological occupation or complex, has helped enormously in establishing their basic order in time. Thin though the information remains for some districts, a picture of developments can now be attempted.

This section concentrates on two groups of people who flourished in the 17th and preceding centuries, knowledge of whom has come to light through such archaeological work. One consists of the irrigation agriculturalists at various places along the foot of the western wall of the Rift, with special attention to those who lived towards the more southerly end in Tanzania, at the remarkable site of Engaruka. The other group is the Sirikwa cattle-keepers in the western highlands of Kenya. After that, a brief conspectus is attempted of the history of the highlands down to the Maasai Revolution of the 17th and 18th centuries. This tries to correlate the archaeological results with other historical evidence (oral, cultural and linguistic) and thus to do justice to some more poorly known, but probably equally important, population groups of that pre-Maasai era.

Before that some explanation would be useful of the prevailing social and political tradition of this region, both since the Maasai Revolution and before it. The contrast with the interlacustrine zone and its kingdoms, which were illustrated in the last section, is very striking.

Government by age-mates

It would be a mistake to assume that the societies of the highlands remained less developed than those of the interlacustrine kingdoms or that their government was on a simpler, smaller scale. The social organization and political systems of the highland peoples – Kalenjin, Maasai, Kikuyu and others – have been as sophisticated and complex as those of any kingdoms. Being for the larger part of a completely different type, one in which the concept of kingship, chieftainship and noble blood is quite alien – so that some anthropologists describe these peoples as 'democratic' – they defy comparison. The central institutions are the age-sets and their continual succession, generation by generation. Each set, or sub-set within it, is formed through the initiation of age-mates on reaching puberty. This normally includes a circumcision ceremony, but comprises in fact much more than that: the circumcision is merely the climax of a lengthy communal and ritual education, as important as any experience in a man's life. It is in essence a process of indoctrination into the mores of the society, emphasising the communal discipline and the loyalty to the age-set of all its members, in times of peaceful herding and in those of warfare and other crises alike. The great ceremonial events in the history of the community are the generational 'hand-overs' of power, when the young 'warrior' set which has recently formed is considered ready to take on the responsibility for the defence of the land and the people, and of course their cattle, while the set ahead moves up into the grade of elderhood. While 'power' is seen to rest with the 'warriors' (*moran* in Maasai), respect is due to the elders. It is the job of the senior (but not too senile) elder set, in its formal and informal councils, to control the younger sets and especially that holding 'power', and to make decisions when necessary for the wellbeing and regulation of the whole community. These include initiation of the next body of youths and the date of the next 'hand-over'.

Social continuity and ideas of history

This regular succession of sets provides a sense of historical continuity to the community. Since events may be remembered as having occurred in the time when this or that set was 'in power', it would seem possible for historians to reconstruct a basic chronology through detailed oral research. Some valuable achievements in this field have indeed been made (on the stages of expansion of the Maasai over two or more centuries for instance), but

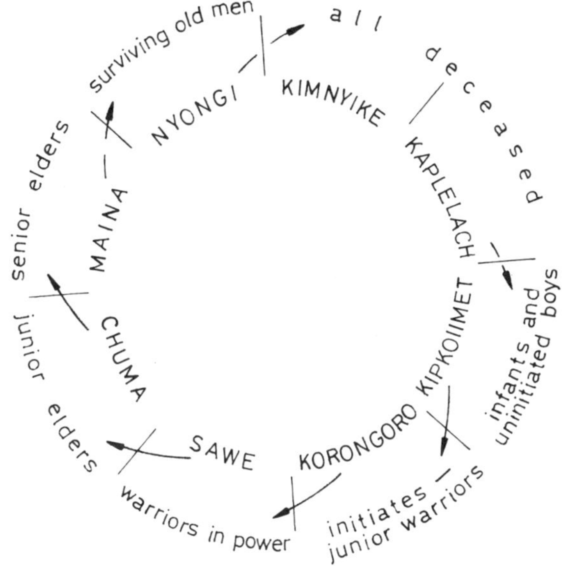

The Kalenjin age-set cycle. As every fifteen or twenty years the set which has newly formed (through the initiation of several sub-sets) takes 'power' at a 'handover' ceremony, each of the sets (inner circle) moves up a grade (outer circle). Thus the Korongoro set, when its initiation period is complete, will be ready to take over 'power', which entails that Sawe, at present in 'power', will move up to junior elderhood. Notice too how the names of deceased sets come up in turn for 'reincarnation'.

often the results have been limited or the order of events unverified. The difficulties revolve around a basic conceptual problem which some modern researchers are slow to appreciate. While each age-set advances, from initiation through warriorhood and power to elderhood and senility until finally all its members pass away, with the next set moving through the same stages a 'generation' behind, these communal institutions are geared to convey a sense of permanence and stability and to deny the idea of real historical motion through time. This is especially so in the Kalenjin system, in which the names of the sets repeat themselves every eight 'generations' (about 150 years in all, it seems). Through such cycling, by which a set is seen not to expire but rather to pass behind in order to reappear at a new dawn, a sense of timeless perpetuity is enshrined. Past events can therefore belong to any time – or all time.

This is of course to simplify and idealise somewhat both the working of government through age systems and these communities' concepts of time and history. Though they have an obvious antiquity, by their nature these systems often inhibit modern historical investigations. Their geographical distribution, from northern Tanzania through the highlands of central Kenya and across the drier plains to southern Ethiopia, also suggests an ancient regional base. Generally they belong to pastoral or pastorally-inclined peoples, non-Bantu in language on the whole, among whom land for grazing is communally owned and managed, and a premium is placed on the cooperation of the age-mates in devising herding strategies and in protecting the stock against diseases and droughts and equally against thieves and enemy forces.

But such generalisations have to admit weighty exceptions, including the age organization of the very numerous Kikuyu and related peoples, who are Bantu in language and decidedly agricultural in the economy which they have developed around Mount Kenya and in the other fertile highlands east of the Rift.

Further south, in the equally fertile forest clearings on the eastern and southern slopes of Kilimanjaro, the dense Chagga population, which has depended on intensive cultivation of bananas and other crops, is also Bantu in linguistic affiliation. They have organised themselves more along lineage than age principles, with allegiance being accorded certain clans and their leaders descending either from those who first cleared individual ridges on the lower slopes, or from those who later consolidated their rule through successful protection of these communities and their land. Similar processes of agricultural settlement and social organization have been nicely illustrated through historical enquiries in the Pare hills stretching southward from Kilimanjaro, and in many districts beyond. Often, as shown in the case of Usambara

(Shambaa), the rulers needed a charismatic reputation enshrined in historical tradition and some form of foundation charter. The story of Mbega makes a classic example.

Historical dynamics of the non-Bantu bulge

The essential elements of social, political and military organization by age-systems must go back beyond the time of the existing communities, to earlier Cushitic-speaking populations of this whole region. The presence of these latter through the Kenyan and northern

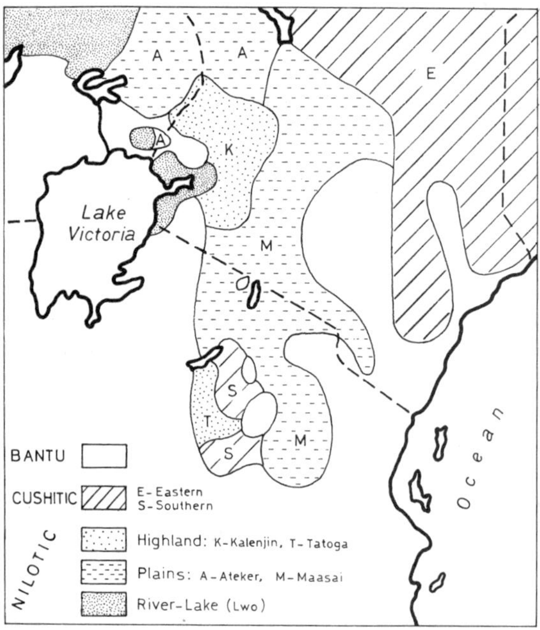

The main language families and their divisions of Uganda, Kenya and Tanzania

Tanzanian highlands from two or three thousand years ago is attested not only by a few remnant Cushitic languages at the southern end of this zone, but also by so much vocabulary of Cushitic derivation in all the existing languages. This applies equally to Highland Bantu (Kikuyu among others) as to Highland Nilotic (Tatoga and Kalenjin) and Plains Nilotic (which includes Maasai). There has thus been a marked degree of cultural and population continuity despite the language changes in this zone.

This linguistic background with its clear message of both a regional tradition and continual changes in the societies of the highlands over the centuries, combined with the archaeological researches described in this section of the book, encourages one to look again at the social systems and their age organization and to press objective historical questions. Simple perusal of old ethnographic literature raises enough to start with. The Kalenjin cycle of age-set names, described above, has in fact its variants. The southerly Kalenjin have suppressed one of the eight names (apparently after a disaster or disgrace, the memory of which it was thought better to extirpate from history). But before that suppression, the eight names, actually reframed as two parallel cycles of four each – a left-hand and a right-hand 'house' – were adopted further south on and beyond the present Kenya-Tanzania border by groups with (now at least) Bantu dialects (Kurya etc). Certain of these set names turn up again far to the east in the generation lists of the Kikuyu and other Mount Kenya people. At the present stage of research, these comparative observations on a regional scale are not fully explained. But they present a challenge, one which shatters the supposition of changelessness over the generations and the centuries which local historical enquiries, respectful to the internal sources, all to easily reproduce.

It is arguable that the recent Kalenjin system has its roots in the Sirikwa era, described below, of three and more centuries ago; thus some of these names which have spread around may derive from that time. But we cannot speculate in detail. That holds even more for the organization of the agricultural villages of Engaruka and related places at the same period. However, the regional background, with the examples of the later irrigation agricultural villages on this western side of the Rift, suggests that old Engaruka would have governed itself through a non-chiefly system, very likely based on some form of succession of age-sets. Essential would have been communal regulation of water-rights and distribution as well as maintenance of the canals and intricate field systems, combined with a disciplined control of residence and stock-management. Existing irrigation communities in this region are highly regulated, and Engaruka, from all the signs which remain on the ground, appears to have been abnormally so.

Irrigation Agriculture at Engaruka

Engaruka lies in thornbush country on the dusty Rift floor, too dry for ordinary agriculture. Both here, however, and at certain other places at the foot of the escarpment, small rivers descend from the wetter Crater Highlands through deeply cut gorges to reach the plain. Some are seasonal; a few, like the Engaruka river, are permanent.

Ancient fields and canals

Between three and six centuries ago the river flows were, as they emerged from the gorges on natural outwash fans, channelled ingeniously into stone-built canals. These were exquisitely levelled, embanked and maintained, some of them running several kilometres along the escarpment base and through the foothills. They were divided and further subdivided into furrows to feed grids of little fields, all carefully stone-walled and levelled. These stone walls and terraces helped conserve the soft dusty soil which was liable, under intensive use, to erode

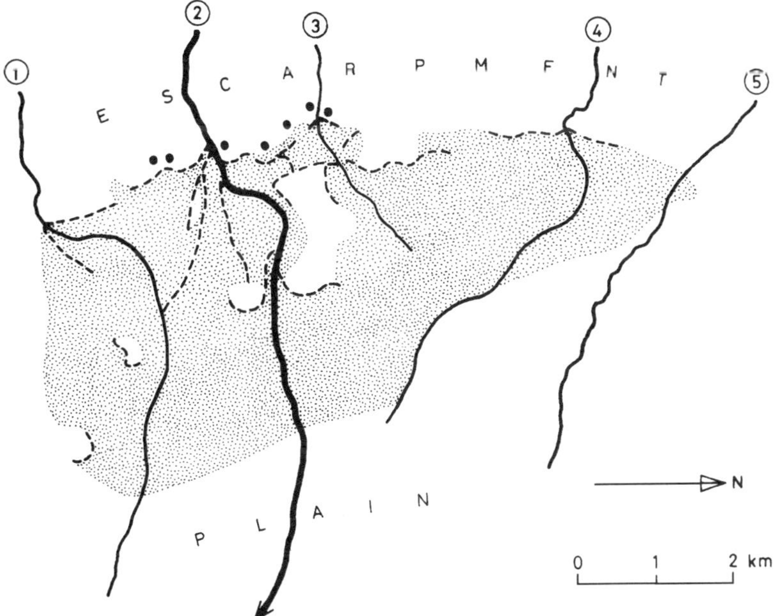

The Engaruka escarpment approached across the Rift floor. (See next page for closer view.) The map shows the minimum extent of ancient fields (shaded), the village sites (black dots) and some of the artery canals (broken lines) led off the small rivers and streams which descended from the highlands through gorges cut in the escarpment. The behaviour of the streams nowadays is as follows:

1. Olemelepo – a flashy stream, opening briefly each rainy season

2. Engaruka – permanent reliable river, usually 3–5 metres broad, excellent water

3. A deep cleft, now dry save for brief flash in occasional years

4. Makuyuni – seasonal flow, four months or more

5. Lolchoro – occasional flow in some or most years

badly into the plain. But equally, the vast numbers of stones on and immediately below the surface dictated that they be lined and piled in the most neat and efficient patterns in order that the land between could be tilled. The main crop was sorghum (*mtama*), charred seeds of which have been found in the hearths of the villages of old Engaruka.

At this site the ancient fields and their irrigation devices can still be seen covering at least 2,000 hectares (5,000 acres) of the escarpment foothills and Rift floor. Several thousand people would have lived here, their houses clustered in seven big and compact villages which were built on the hillsides in series of steep terraces just above the highest fields and artery canals. They kept some cattle, as well as goats and sheep, in stalls within the villages and in stone enclosures constructed in the field area. Here the stock would normally have been stall-fed, since the intensity of cultivation would have prohibited free grazing. In return the animal manure, carefully treated and applied, would have helped maintain the fertility and yields of the intensively cultivated plots. Altogether then, the evidence derived from the abandoned fields and irrigation works and from the villages provides a picture of an unusually specialised and integrated agricultural economy.

Desertion of Engaruka

About 1700 AD Engaruka's fields and villages were abandoned – as were several similar sites by Lakes Eyasi, Manyara and Natron. The reasons for this desertion are not yet fully understood. It is known that Maasai were moving into the region about that time. But there is no evidence that they drove out the old Engaruka people; on the contrary, pastoral Maasai have usually found it advantageous to tolerate agricultural settlements in their midst provided competition for water and grazing is not too fierce.

More probably Engaruka was in the long run the victim of its own success in exploiting a very special and restricted situation. With the population increasing over several generations, at some point the absolute limits of both water and irrigable land would have been reached. Pressure to produce yet more would have led inevitably to soil-exhaustion and declining harvests, despite all the technological ingenuity of the community. They had in a sense over-specialised and found themselves eventually at their wits' end.

Gradual though the crisis may have been, eventually the strain was too severe and the community broke up. The remnants dispersed and would have been assimilated piecemeal among various surrounding peoples in northern Tanzania. A contributory factor in the collapse must have been decline in the river flows. Some of those from which irrigation canals were once led, and on which large areas of the fields were dependent, are now dry or far too unreliable.

Whatever the eventual explanation, it will not be simple. One wonders about climatic change: there are indeed suggestions that south of the Equator a wetter period around the 15th–16th centuries was followed by a generally drier trend in the 17th and 18th. But even if that

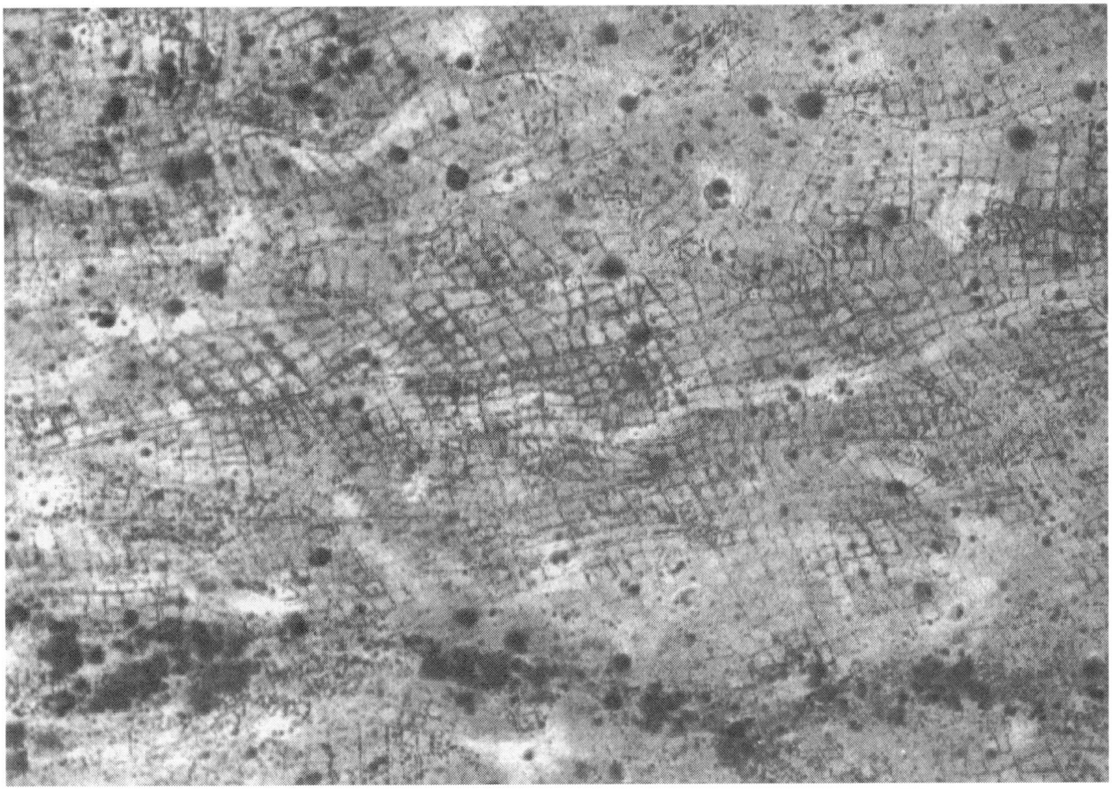

Grids of stone-divided fields and irrigation canals at Engaruka photographed from the air (above, Tanzania Survey), and from the escarpment foot (below).

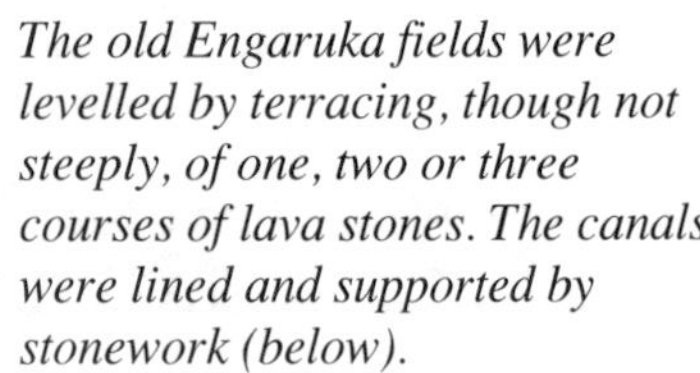

The old Engaruka fields were levelled by terracing, though not steeply, of one, two or three courses of lava stones. The canals were lined and supported by stonework (below).

If there were still too many stones on the field surface, they were neatly piled – and the heap revetted almost vertically – in the corner of the field (bottom).

should be confirmed, it is unlikely to be the sole explanation of the deterioration of the Engaruka escarpment's hydrology. For one thing, if the period of Engaruka's flowering had been significantly wetter, the inhabitants would not have been stimulated to develop and maintain such an elaborate irrigation system for their fields. One speculation is that this settled community of several thousand would, over a number of generations, have had an adverse effect on the environment, especially in cutting wood on the escarpment for building and for fuel, thus damaging the stream catchments.

Excavations in one of the villages of old Engaruka by Hamo Sassoon: platform enclosure and gateway for house (above); outdoor fireplace (below). (Scale: one metre in 10 cm sections.)

History of irrigation: Sonjo and Kilimanjaro

Although Engaruka eventually collapsed, its tradition is not entirely dead. Part of it has survived at Sonjo, a hundred kilometres northwards above Lake Natron. The Sonjo fields and furrows are not exact replicas: in particular they lack the intricate stonework of Engaruka. In general the Sonjo agricultural system is less intensive, lacking cattle and therefore manuring too. On the other hand the old Engaruka villages – which several archaeologists have investigated, notably Louis Leakey in 1935, Hamo Sassoon of the Tanzanian Antiquities in 1964 and 1966, and Peter Robertshaw and the British Institute in 1982 – would have looked very similar to recent Sonjo ones. Some specific details, such as the outdoor fireplaces, are identical, showing that part – but only a part – of the ancestry of Sonjo derives from the Engaruka people. There are differences too: the pots used by the Engaruka farmers contrasted in detail with those nowadays made and used in the Sonjo villages.

Ancient irrigation was not confined to this one escarpment. Well to the east – on Kilimanjaro, in the Pare and Taita hills and in some basins below – there is a long tradition which still thrives of combining artificial irrigation with rainfed cultivation. Here the reason for irrigation is not so much lack of rain in those fertile hills as the density of population to be fed, necessitating extension of planting into the drier season. In other words there has over several centuries been a spiralling effect of suitable conditions, population increase and local ingenuity to provide supplementary water supplies for growing enough food. On Kilimajaro in particular shortage of land and the need to maintain fertility have led – as at Engaruka – to confining of cattle in stalls and carrying fodder to them from afar, and in return the use of their manure on the fields. These instances of irrigation and intensive cultivation systems east of the Rift may be historically connected with Engaruka, or they could have evolved independently. The situations are different; so are the details of the fields and canals.

Marakwet

Better existing parallels for the intricacies of the Engaruka irrigation can be seen over 400 kilometres northward in Kenya, again on the steep Rift escarpment and its foot, in Marakwet and adjacent districts flanking the Kerio valley. Here again the whole system of land-

A Sonjo village with its defended gateway and round houses built on platform-terraces.

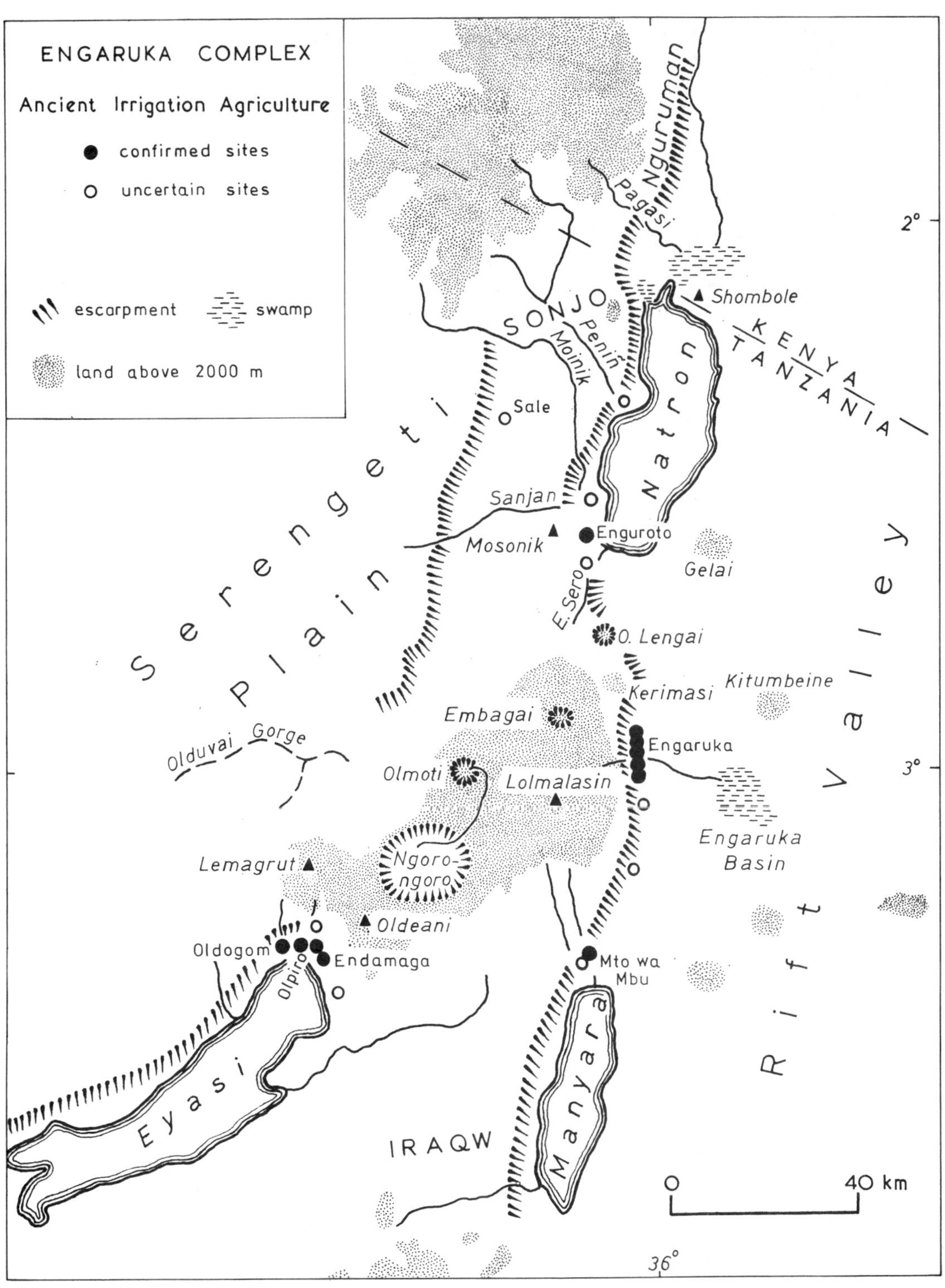
ENGARUKA COMPLEX
Ancient Irrigation Agriculture
confirmed sites
uncertain sites
escarpment
swamp
land above 2000 m
Nguruman
Pagasi
2°
Shombole
SONJO
Penin
Moinik
KENYA
TANZANIA
Natron
Sale
Serengeti Plain
Sanjan
Mosonik
Enguroto
Gelai
E. Sero
O. Lengai
Kerimasi
Kitumbeine
Embagai
Engaruka
Olduvai Gorge
Olmoti
Lolmalasin
3°
Engaruka Basin
Lemagrut
Ngoro-ngoro
Oldeani
Oldogom
Olpiro
Endamaga
Mto wa Mbu
Rift Valley
Eyasi
IRAQW
Manyara
0
40 km
36°

An irrigation canal being led from the Embobut river along the escarpment face to water the fields of Endo in Marakwet.

use and the location of settlements are determined by the rivers tumbling from the forested highlands and by the artificial distribution of water on the drier terrain below.

Local tradition insists that the Marakwet irrigation is ancient and evolved locally. There is no evidence to suggest the contrary, although disbelieving voices are heard occasionally. More than a century back, the Scotsman Joseph Thomson, leading the Royal Geographical Society's expedition across Maasailand to Lake Victoria, encountered the Marakwet stretch of the escarpment on his return journey. He liked to colour his descriptions, to the extent of mixing biblical similes:

> We were almost baffled in our attempt to descend, owing to the excessive steepness of the way, and the loose blocks which strewed the face of the mountain. I here noticed the employment of canals for irrigation, on a larger scale than in Teita, many of them being conveyed with surprising judgement along the most unexpected places. We contrived to make the descent without accident, and the men camped beside one of the artificial canals employed to bring the water from a great distance, to irrigate the ground at the base. In camping here, we found we had simply delivered ourselves into the hands of the Philistines. The natives at once put the screw upon us to extort a large hongo. Seeing us hesitate, they quietly retired, and the water with them – for they could easily divert it in its upper course. This was quite sufficient to produce the desired effect. We humbly paid up; and immediately, as if a modern rod of Moses had struck the rock, the water began to flow.
>
> (*Through Masai Land*, 1885, p. 310.)

It has yet to be proved that the Marakwet and Engaruka systems of irrigation agriculture are historically related. But they share certain points, especially of canal construction techniques on the escarpment. So the argument is, to say the least, attractive for imagining an early extension along the Rift Valley of grain-cultivators with a locally evolved irrigation technology, well before the big changes of the 17th and 18th centuries.

The Sirikwa livestock specialists

Five-hundred years ago the whole of Kenya's western highlands, between Sotik and Mount Elgon and eastwards as far as Nakuru, was the territory of the Sirikwa. These people are thought to be ancestral, broadly speaking, to the present Kalenjin (some of them however being absorbed into Luyia and Maasai). Although nowa-

Though unspectacular and rarely photogenic even when cleared of bush and long grass, Sirikwa Holes are obvious archaeological features on the landscape. This example, photographed in the early 1960s, is one of a large group at Kabiyet in northern Nandi.

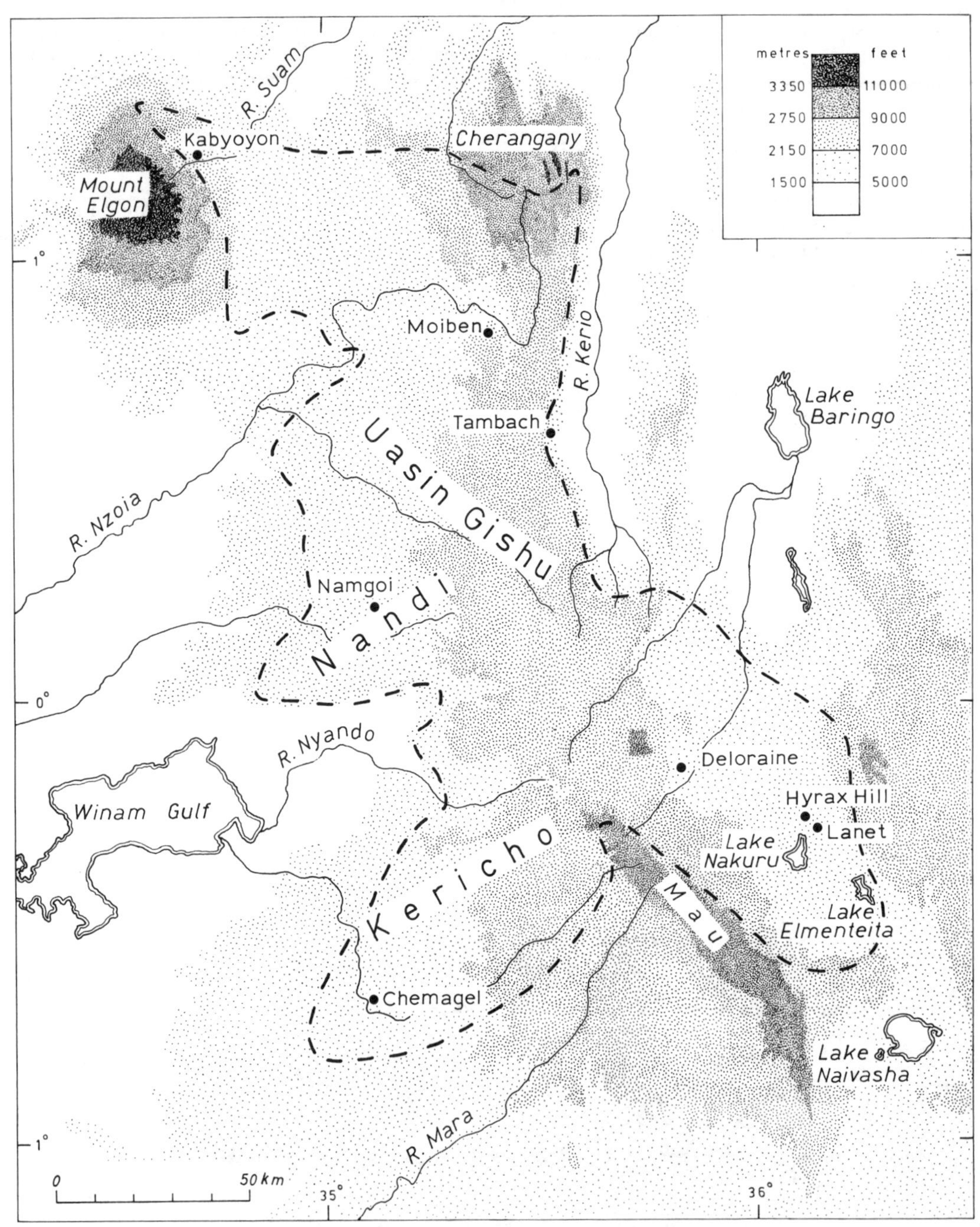

The Sirikwa zone in the Western Highlands and Central Rift of Kenya, between the 12th and 18th centuries approximately. The limits are indicated by the broken line; excavated Sirikwa Holes are marked and named.

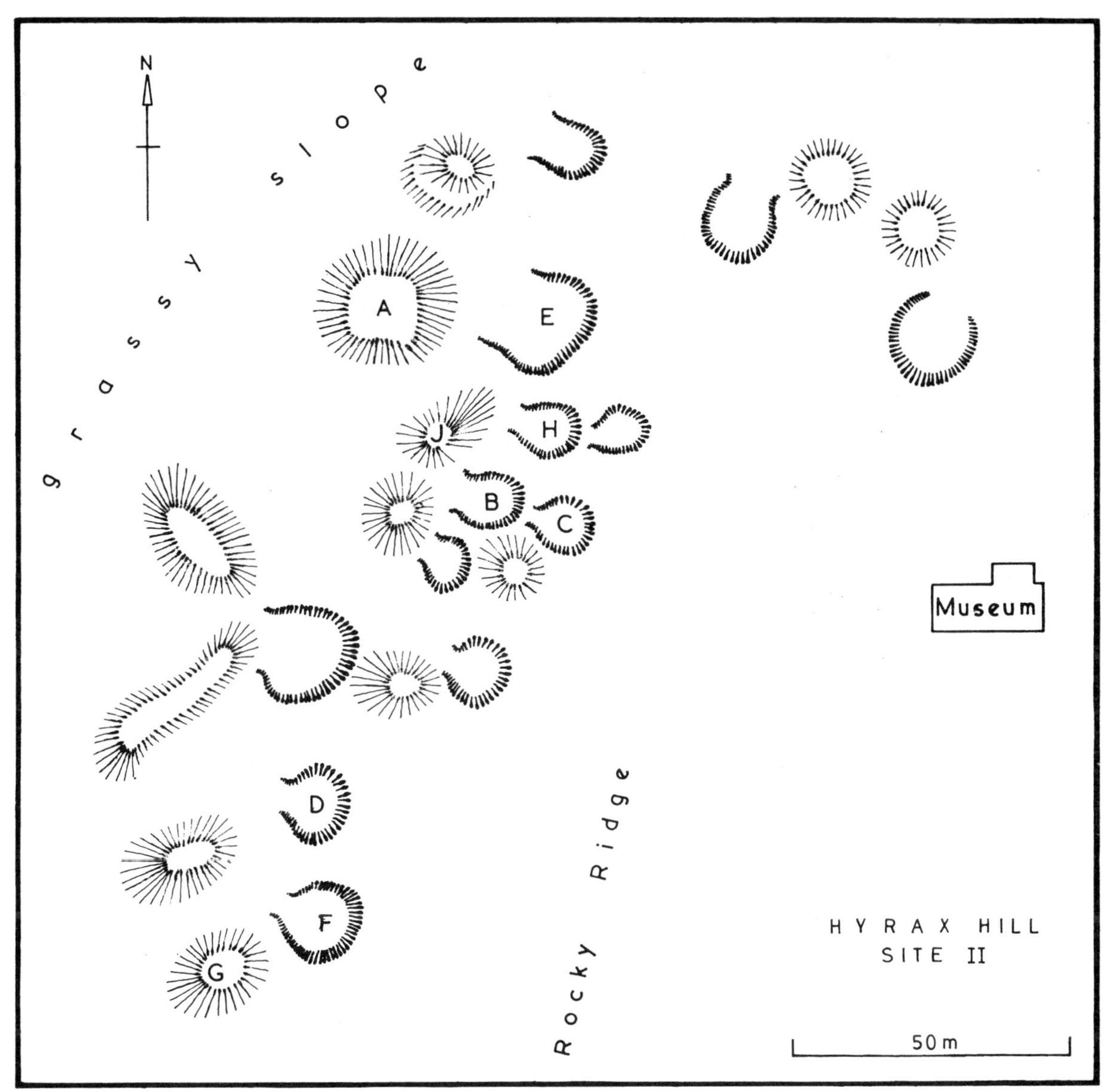

Hyrax Hill, Site II – a group of thirteen Sirikwa Holes and associated mounds (after Dr Mary Leakey). Excavations in Sirikwa Holes B, C, D, E, and F and in associated mounds A, G and J have been undertaken in 1938 (by Mary Leakey), 1964 (by the Kenya Museums) and 1985 (by the British Institute). Some of the finds from this and other archaeological sites in the Central Rift are kept in the museum, converted from an old farm-house, at Hyrax Hill.

The reconstruction (p.51) is based on the excavation of Sirikwa Hole F (with Mound G) in 1985.

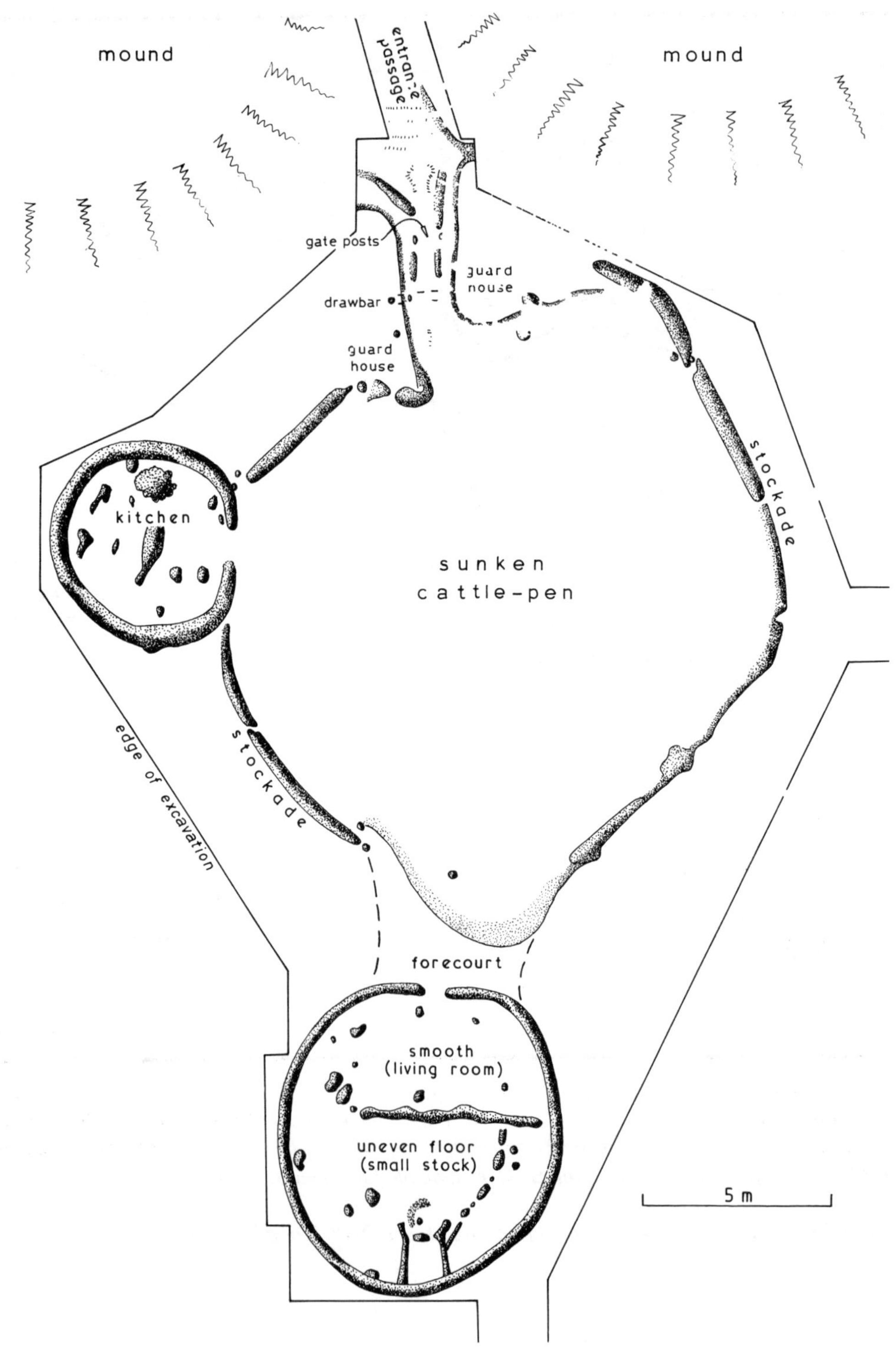
mound
entrance passage
mound
gate posts
guard house
drawbar
guard house
kitchen
sunken cattle-pen
stockade
stockade
edge of excavation
forecourt
smooth (living room)
uneven floor (small stock)
5 m

A large Sirikwa Hole excavated at Chemagel (Sotik), near the southern end of the zone. This is a late example, perhaps only 200 years old. The view is from the uphill end. The plan and the wide photograph (taken before the control cross-baulks were removed) show the round hollowed cattle-pen and surrounding trench for a stockade, and at the downhill extremity the narrow gateway with guard-posts on either side, and beyond that the approach passage curving between the mounds of piled dung.

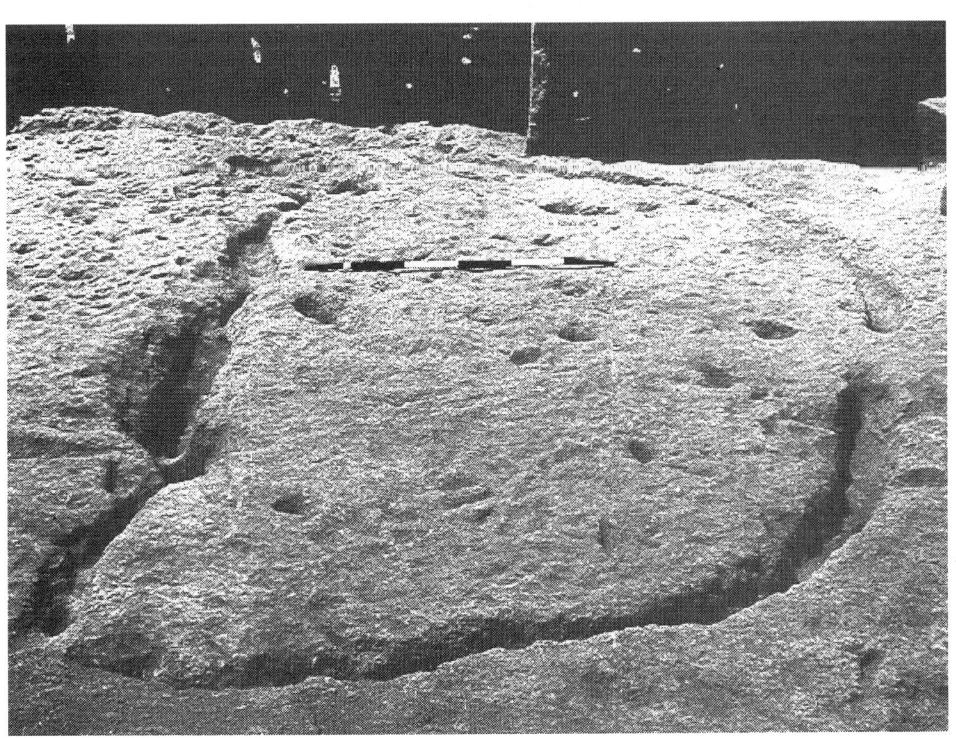

The larger of two attached houses, that at the back, with its internal divisions, is seen in the foreground, and in the separate photograph taken after the completion of the excavation. (Scale in feet, the rod measuring nearly two metres overall.) This house may have been not so dissimilar from recent Kalenjin houses in the western highlands of Kenya (see over). However, the wall construction with continuous posts would have been different.

Kalenjin houses in Cherangany and on the Elgeyo escarpment, the latter under construction, the wall frame still to be daubed

days no-one calls himself Sirikwa, the memory of that period is very much alive, with the signs of ancient activity remaining so clear on the ground. Anyone who has stayed or travelled in Kericho, Nandi, Uasin Gishu and adjacent districts will have noticed the saucer-shaped depressions, each ten metres or so wide, known as 'Sirikwa Holes'. They occur on the hillsides in groups numbering anything between five and fifty, sometimes even a hundred. Often covered with grass or bush, or with big trees standing in them, their antiquity is obvious enough.

Fifty years of research

Among the early investigators of these archaeological features was G.W.B. Huntingford, a local schoolteacher who undertook some remarkably informative surveys and descriptions in Nandi and Uasin Gishu in the 1920s. But the first serious excavations of Sirikwa Holes were those of Mary Leakey on Hyrax Hill by Nakuru in 1938. Several others were investigated, mostly by the British Institute in Eastern Africa, between 1957 and 1964 – at Lanet, Kabyoyon (by Suam), Kapsabet, Tambach, Moiben and Chemagel (Sotik). Each excavation has increased our knowledge both of the detailed form and structure of Sirikwa Holes and of the cultural and economic history of the region. Renewed work at Hyrax Hill in 1985–86, followed up at the Deloraine site at Rongai in the same district, has been especially enlightening.

Chemegel Sirikwa Hole: cutting through the entrance passage and the flanking dung-heaps

Reconstruction through excavation

These hollows – 'holes' is really the wrong word – were known to represent the cattle-pens of the old Sirikwa, according to Kalenjin elders. The recent archaeological excavations have vindicated this testimony. They had been deliberately hollowed out and stoutly fenced – stockaded rather – all round. The narrow entrance always faced downhill and was protected by a strong gate, and sometimes a drawbar too, with guard-points inside. In rocky terrain – in Uasin Gishu, upper Elgeyo and parts of Nandi – neat dry-stone walling substituted for the fence or provided supports for fence and gate alike. No houses stood inside: the hollowed enclosure was open to the sky. Houses there were of course, but outside, against the fence.

The houses, which numbered one, two or three with each Sirikwa Hole, were an integral part of the complex. They had no separate approach; they were entered through the main gate and the hollowed cattle-pen, a small gap in the fence being at the same time the house door. The house shape was roundish, but not always perfectly circular. Some were only three metres wide, sufficient for a herdboy and a calf or two, separated by a rough partition across the middle of the house. Others were twice as broad, to accommodate a family. These too were usually divided into two or more rooms, one half with a smooth floor being for living and sleeping, the other, whose floor became rough and pitted, for small stock and calves (which would have been crushed if left at night with the adult cattle in the open hollow).

House construction

Some of these bigger houses may have resembled later Kalenjin ones with wooden and daubed walls and a thatch frame above, in other words the basic 'cone-on-cylinder' type found throughout the highlands. But the smaller houses would have been of dome or 'beehive' shape, with flimsy arched walls and grass covering. In the Nakuru district they were sometimes built in pairs to flank the entrance of the hollow, each house door thus serving as a sentry-point on the inner side of the gate.

A peculiarity of all Sirikwa houses is seen in the foundations for the walls (both external ones and internal partitions). These do not consist of individual post-holes; instead they take the form of a continuous trench, apparently chipped in the sub-soil and rock with a small hoe. One such with a worn blade was found by Merrick Posnansky when excavating close to Sirikwa Holes at Lanet, a group only four km from Hyrax Hill (p.52).

Economy

With its house or houses then, a Sirikwa Hole formed a closed unit with a single, guarded means of access approached from below. Each day the cattle were taken out, following which the dung and mud were removed, and, together with domestic rubbish and ash, thrown onto a heap shortly below the entrance. These heaps were sometimes strategically placed to hide the gate from view, and in Kericho district they accumulated in pairs, flanking the curving hollowed passage which led to the gate. They account for the grassy 'humps and bumps' which are usually visible among groups of Sirikwa Holes.

Excavating a stone-revetted Sirikwa Hole at Moiben, on the north side of the Uasin Gishu plateau, looking downhill into the entrance enclosure. Though the size is much smaller than that of the Chemagel example, the attached house at the back more flimsy and modest, and the stone walls (doubtless surmounted by a thorn fence) substituting for a stockade, the essential features are identical. This example dates about the 16th century.

Below: detail of dry-stone revetting with rather shapeless lava boulders, one split in half to obtain smooth faces. (Scale divided by feet; each rod measuring nearly two metres overall.) The fallen stones in foreground show that the original height was about twice that preserved.

The Sirikwa were by no means the first pastoralists to exploit these fine high grasslands. The keeping of cattle, and also of goats and sheep, was already two-thousand years old in this particular region. But it seems that the Sirikwa were the first to perfect a specialised form of dairy pastoralism, combining milk cattle with flocks of goats and sheep for the regular supply of meat for roasting. The breed of cattle which they selected for this purpose and improved in these lush highland pastures was distinctly humped, but smaller and much shorter-horned than that of the interlacustrine zone. Similar herd and flock management systems were later adopted here by several sections of the Maasai who benefitted from the Sirikwa experience. The difference, as explained below, is that the Maasai success in maintaining such a way of living was based on new social and military organization combined with more effective tactics of warfare and raiding, of attack and defence, with bigger iron spears.

Not all the Sirikwa maintained themselves exclusively as herders. They were certainly not nomadic, even though they would have sent their young men with the herds out to seasonal grazing in Uasin Gishu and Nakuru. Some of them, at least the later Sirikwa, depended partly on grains, especially in the wetter districts of Nandi and Kericho (where their Kalenjin descendants have maintained this tradition of a mixed economy). Here one finds not only grindstones and more cooking pots – of the distinctive Sirikwa-Kalenjin style – but also more substantial and permanent houses attached to the Sirikwa Holes. These comprised family homesteads. Honey obtained from the forest-dwelling Okiek was doubtless important too, especially for beer.

Population

Sirikwa Holes run to thousands upon thousands, as one begins to realise on attempting detailed local surveys. Such enormous numbers can give a false impression of former population density. It must be remembered that they were being continually constructed and abandoned over several centuries, from about the 12th till the 18th; what we see now is the accumulated record. In fact each family would have needed a new cattle-pen every five or so years – as the fence timbers rotted, and the house structures deteriorated, or the dung-heap reached an uncomfortable size. Thus in each generation every Sirikwa family left its mark on the landscape several times. All the same, the digging of the hollows into the hillsides and the construction of the stockades and entrance devices would have been laborious tasks. Presumably the labour was organised communally through an age-set system, probably not so different institutionally from those of later peoples of this region. But the scale of this mobilisation of labour, both for constructing Sirikwa Holes and for herding and defence, would seem to have been more modest and local than among the more wide-ranging pastoralists of the last two-hundred years.

Time of change

During the 17th and 18th centuries Sirikwa Holes ceased to be made as homestead arrangements and devices for guarding livestock. The simple reason for this must be new methods of attack with bigger-scale cattle-raiding. For Sirikwa Holes had been designed as protection not against armies, but against small stealthy bands of rustlers. Once large bodies of organised far-ranging cattle-raiders threatened, ready to break or burn defences and challenging to a fight, Sirikwa Holes were rendered vulnerable, indeed useless. Different, more mobile techniques of protecting stock had now to be devised. Later, the favourite system was to relay the alarm from ridge to ridge across the pastures so that the herds could be combined and run into the forest glades where the enemy, should he dare pursue, would be ambushed by concealed archers. Thus larger-scale communal methods of attack were countered by a revolution in the scale and organization of defensive tactics.

These changes were part of a broader transformation taking place in herding strategies, social organization and military techniques and weaponry across a large part of East Africa. Connected with this was the emergence of the Maasai as a power, and their successful establishment as the dominant herdsmen of the fine high pastures of Kenya and northern Tanzania. But the Maasai were not the cause of it all: that confederation was just one symptom of a revolutionary situation some 250 years ago.

Reconstruction of an early Sirikwa Hole of about 1200 AD at Hyrax Hill by Nakuru, near the south-easterly limit of the Sirikwa range.

The reconstruction is based entirely on the evidence obtained by excavating in and around the hollow as well as in the mound to the side of the entrance. The latter consisted mostly of dung, but contained also rubbish. This included broken pots used for storage of water and probably beer, not for cooking, as well as food refuse in the form of bones of small humped cattle, goats and sheep. The meat had been roasted. The cattle were for the most part, it seems, kept for their milk.

The excavations have revealed the form of the open-air hollow with its surrounding stockade trench (for the most part a step-trench, the posts being supported by packed stones on the inner side – see top photo), the narrow gateway between two small elliptical houses, and the form and internal divisions of these and of the one additional house. All three houses were entered through the hollow, an arrangement found consistently in Sirikwa Holes.

Each of these houses was divided into three or four rooms, the front part with heavily pitted floors being for calves and small stock, the back partition for living, eating (a small hearth being clear in each) and sleeping (in the room with a smooth surface, skins doubtless being used for both mattress and blankets). See the two lower photographs.

Photographic scales, both one-metre and half-metre, are in 10 cm sections.

These houses, probably of low curving profile and flimsy materials, would have looked considerably different from the substantial ones attached to the late Sirikwa Hole at Chemagel (see illustrations on pp.44–46). That would have been a permanent family base; this Nakuru example by contrast appears to have been a pastoral encampment, though by no means a mere temporary camp.

In excavating the wooden wall line of a house attached to a Sirikwa Hole on Deloraine Farm at Rongai near Nakuru, the actual chip-marks cut in the soft lava rock when preparing the foundation trench were found preserved. (The trowel is for scale: the metal blade measures 10 cm.)

An iron tool, perhaps similar to the small worn chipping hoe (17 cm long) found at the Sirikwa site of Lanet, also by Nakuru, would have been used.

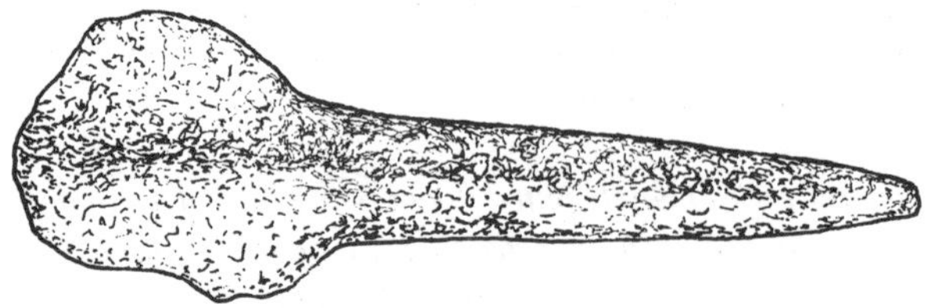

The Maasai Revolution and beyond

One aspect of this revolution, essential to the Maasai ascendancy, needs underlining however. That is the power of iron. The metal had of course been known and used since long before; yet the Sirikwa and other early pastoralists in these highlands had exploited it on a relatively light scale. Despite their elaborate construction activity, their iron requirements did not compare with those of agricultural populations living to their east and west. The Maasai era was accompanied by obvious intensification of demand for iron in the pastures, as part of the new scale and methods of warfare and raiding and equally of defence. In particular, big socketed spears became fashionable, so that those who could obtain or afford only the older lighter varieties, which were hafted into the wooden shaft by means of a tang, found themselves pushed off the best plateau grasslands and confined to broken peripheral districts. Success in this new situation was dependent on a corps of craftsmen who could smelt larger quantities of iron and produce armaments of unprecedented size and quality. This meant conscripting the services of iron-working clans whose specialist role in relation to the herdsmen was perpetuated from generation to generation. The iron-workers of this region, in contrast to those further west and south, did not carry a high prestige in society at large. Sometimes they are described as despised or even 'outcaste', and those born into these particular families found it difficult to escape from the profession. But, fulfilling as they did such essential functions for the cattle-keepers, they were feared for their powers and respected for their skills and products. So the artisan could in fact feel as proud of himself and his family as could the most celebrated warrior or the richest owner of cows and goats.

Cultivators and herdsmen

> They are mostly warlike nomads, with a social system based on military ideals, who were long the terror and scourge of all their neighbours. They recognise only two things as worthy of their care and interest, namely cattle and warfare. (Sir Charles Eliot, *The East African Protectorate*, 1905, p.134.)

Eliot, one of the first British governors of Kenya, was by no means unintelligent. His account, for those who read on thoughtfully, contains valuable insights. But for many

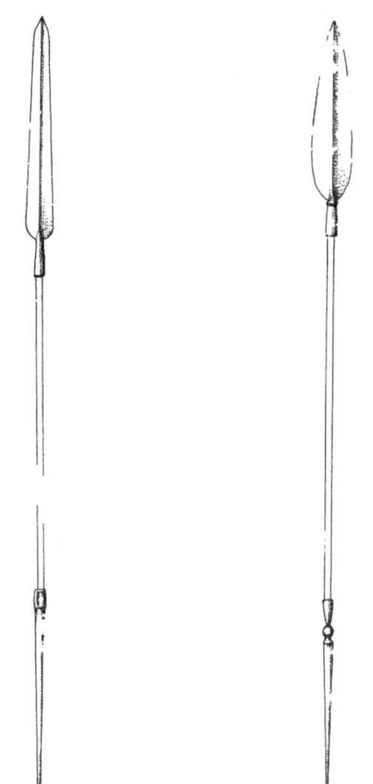

Socketed and weighted spears of northern (left) and southern Maasai as illustrated by Thomson in the 1880s.

readers he echoed – and added authority to – the popular image of the Maasai as a warlike, terrorising and purely pastoral nation, living off the meat of their herds and flocks and the milk of their cattle (sometimes mixed with blood). This simplistic view – or 'myth' of the Maasai – has in recent years been attacked by a number of anthropologists and historians. Certain Maasai sections have, it is true, succeeded in maintaining a pastoral life without cultivating at all and by refusing to accept grain, vegetables and game-meat of any sort (in theory, if not always in practice through droughts and times of severe losses of stock). But the size of population that the fine grasslands can support on such a diet is limited, the amounts of milk and meat being determined by the extent and quality of the grass itself.

Thus, in the 19th century, Maasai sections fought other Maasai for control of the best tracts of grazing. Such competition for territory and its defence were the basic causes of the inter-Maasai wars; raiding for milch-cows and breeding bulls, of which one hears so much, was definitely secondary in importance to this – essential though such action might be for restocking and pastoral survival after disease or drought had decimated one's herd.

From time to time therefore whole Maasai sections, to south and north alike, were forced off the fine plateaus into inferior grazing lands where they had to devise mutually acceptable exchange and territorial arrangements with settled agricultural people. In each generation moreover a number of Maasai individuals, of poor parentage or large families unable to bequeath an adequate herd, took the option of going to live with such cultivators and marrying there. Where sufficient numbers did this they founded agricultural Maasai communities, in some instances employing irrigation techniques to ensure a harvest year by year. Certain of these – the Arush below Mount Meru, the Nguruman next to Sonjo and the Njemps by Lake Baringo – came to specialise in supplying caravans late in the 19th century.

It was therefore only a minority of the Maasai which in the long run succeeded in maintaining the ideal of the purely pastoral life. In fact this ideal of Maasainess – and the associated claim of 'pure' Maasai descent – were exaggerated at a late stage of history by the successful minority. Forming in a loose way a central pastoral Maasai confederation, these sections sought to justify their control of the finest pastures and to distance themselves historically from their brethren.

Such cultural and economic diversity has parallels – though not of course exact ones – in pre-Maasai times some three and more centuries back. For, as seen, the Sirikwa had been varied and adaptable in the western highlands, more so than the obvious signs of their own pastoral ideal might at first sight suggest.

They would have been moreover well aware of the cultivators on their north-eastern margin using irrigation at the foot of the Kerio escarpment, what is now Marakwet. Relations were probably quite close – as they can often be between peoples with contrasting ways of living which provide opportunities for exchange. In bad years in the high grasslands, when low rainfall reduced the growth of grass and hence the milk yields, many Sirikwa would doubtless have looked to this side for agricultural supplement. Some Sirikwa apparently settled there, becoming thereby less Sirikwa of course; it was probably in this way that the Kerio valley became in time

Kalenjin-speaking. There were other cultivators on the western side of the plateau, that is in the lower country towards Lake Victoria. These spoke Bantu languages of the Luyia group and had close relations with the Sirikwa. In fact they intermixed considerably, some of the northerly Luyia clans towards Mount Elgon recalling a Sirikwa past.

Pastoralists of the Serengeti side

The Sirikwa would not have had direct contact with the more southerly of the rift-wall irrigation cultivators, those of Nguruman, Sonjo and Engaruka. Between them, herding the Loita-Mara plains of south-eastern Kenya and the Serengeti beyond, were the Tatoga. One section of the latter thrived in the Crater Highlands above Engaruka. These Tatoga were related linguistically to the Sirikwa, but in these more southerly grasslands they organised their herding strategies differently. They constructed nothing comparable to Sirikwa Holes there. However, when the Sirikwa way of living was phased out in the 18th century, so in these high plains to the south did the Tatoga break up. Their territory became that of better organised pastoral Maasai. Many Tatoga were Maasaiized, that is became incorporated into these successful Maasai sections. The remnants retreated yet further southwards into scattered or inferior grasslands of north-central Tanzania, where their descendants still herd cattle and speak the Tatoga tongue.

Tsetse, cattle diseases and history

In many such lower pastures and along the highland fringes of this region – as equally in the interlacustrine one – cattle-keepers had to be on their guard against tsetse-fly and the fatal trypanosomiasis parasites. The tsetse zones are not stable; they are liable to shift, expand and contract for a variety of reasons. It is not simply a matter of the fly forcing cattle and their keepers off certain grazings; it has often been the absence of cattle for a short period, following a devastating disease and heavy mortality in the herds, which has allowed the pasture to deteriorate, let in the ranker grasses and bush, and created an environment in which tsetse can thrive. Such constraints have not been encountered in the cooler highlands (or in the more arid parts of the plains to the north). Thus, while cattle have long been kept by agricultural populations in many other regions of East Africa, it is in these high open grasslands adjoining the Rift Valley that pastoralism has enjoyed both scale and continuity by helping to create and maintain over three millennia its own environment.

Cultivators crossing the Rift

In pre-Maasai times, then, the Tatoga adjoined the Sirikwa Kalenjin around Chepalungu and Sotik, to the west of the high Mau forest. One very interesting development, poorly recognised by historians though it is, occurred along this cultural boundary, or perhaps by squeezing through the narrow corridor between the zones. This was an agricultural settlement process of Bantu cultivators from the eastern highlands around Mount Kenya (the early Kikuyu-Kamba-Meru group essentially) westwards across the Rift to the edges of the Mau forest. It proceeded further west and south-west into what has become the country of the Gusii and Kurya. Here they mixed with other Bantu groups long settled around Lake Victoria; the present languages bear testimony to this dual ancestry.

Some of these settlers of eastern origin combined with the southerly Sirikwa: the big Sirikwa Holes of Sotik district, revealing a combination of cattle-keeping and cultivation, seem to illustrate this. Somewhere in this one might locate the clues to the sharing of age-set names between Kalenjin and various Bantu people either side of the Rift. In changing situations, such intermixture and adaptation could often prove the most successful option.

Another example of Bantu from the eastern highlands crossing the Rift and successfully combining with an existing population is seen in the Sonjo case above Lake Natron, where they have built nucleated villages and cultivated by irrigation. As explained earlier, the irrigation tradition and perhaps an equal part of the Sonjo ancestry derive from the Engaruka people who were not Bantu-speaking. It was doubtless something in this combination which helped Sonjo to adapt and survive while Engaruka and similar settlements to the south expired.

Adaptation and assimilation

The Engaruka people – whose language was almost certainly of the Cushitic family which was once widespread in the East African highlands but is now very restricted

– had developed, as shown, a very distinct culture and specialised economy. So in a very different way had the Sirikwa – whose unrelated language should be classified as Highland Nilotic, in effect old Kalenjin. But neither lived in isolation (rather cut off from other cultivators though the Engaruka people found themselves). Their histories, both while they thrived and when they were eventually phased out, are to be understood in the context of the surrounding peoples with whom they interacted. While many of these to east and west were Bantu-speakers, there were, to the north and north-east of the highlands, other, largely pastoral, peoples, some with Nilotic languages, though of a very distinct division of that family. From one of these arose the Maasai. But, as seen, the existing Maasai derive as much from the various people whom they assimilated in the high grasslands, as Maasai power became dominant and their way of living prestigious. This is what happened to many of the Tatoga and to certain Sirikwa outliers and splinters. While the new Maasai system depended on more effective methods of stock-management and protection, the ecological knowledge necessary for grazing successfully in the fine high grasslands of the Rift and westerly plateaus was handed down from these indigenous populations, elements of whom became in time thoroughly incorporated within the Maasai ethnicity.

The northern factor

This enlargement of the Maasai into the highlands from a northerly direction, no later than the 18th century, invites one to consider what was happening in those drier plains between the Kenyan and the Ethiopian highlands. Another remarkable example of expansion and incorporation, but in different directions, had taken place a little earlier. This was the Galla – or Oromo as most divisions of that people call themselves – maintaining, like the Maasai, a pastoral ideal, armed with heavy iron spears and large tough shields, and organised in age-sets. During the 16th century Galla groups penetrated into the heart of the Ethiopian empire in one direction and as far as the northern Swahili coast in the other, thus making themselves the scourge of settled Muslim and Christian communities at the same time.

An Ethiopian priest or monk, who signed himself Bahrey, wrote in 1593 a valuable if unsympathetic account of these 'bad and barbaric people', the 'enemies of religion' – who had *inter alia* looted his own home in the south of Ethiopia. He noted the division of the Galla into left- and right-hand moieties, called Baretuma and Boran – names which remain current, albeit with somewhat modified connotations, 400 years later. Especially instructive is his explanation of their age-set system, after which he proceeded to tell the history of Galla raids into Ethiopia from the early 16th century, set by set.

> They have neither king nor master like other peoples, but they obey the *luba* for a period of eight years, at the end of which another *luba* is made and the first gives up his office. They do this at fixed times; and *luba* means 'those who are circumcised together'. The law concerning their circumcision is that when a *luba* is formed they all give themselves a collective name (just as the king of Ethiopia's regiments give themselves each a praise-name).
>
> The translation of Bahrey's Ethiopic text is taken from C.F. Beckingham and G.W.B. Huntingford, *Some Records of Ethiopia, 1593-1646* (Hakluyt Society, 2nd series, CVII), 1954, p.115.

The allusion to obeying the *luba* till he gives up office refers to the leader elected by the set for its eight-year term of military eminence and 'power'. In the highlands to the south, the sets of the Kalenjin, Kikuyu, Maasai and others have not been so short; they approach generational length (15, 20 or more years). But the principles of formation and hand-over are similar, as is the institutional centrality of the age system to the community as a whole. The functions of sets are much more than military; but in times of prolonged warfare and preparedness, whether for aggression and expansion or conversely for defence of the herds and the pastures and the homesteads, the social and political role of the age-set system becomes obviously enhanced and geared to military requirements. Not uncommonly in such tense situations charismatic leaders, sometimes described as 'prophets', arise and extend their grip over the warrior set and its actions.

Such systems of organising society could not have been suddenly invented. In the broad region between the Kenyan and the Ethiopian highlands they must be much older than the Galla (Oromo) expansion of the 16th century. But that episode may represent a revival of this form of government and a sharpening of its elements in a situation of new pressures affecting people with a pastoral base. The Maasai phenomenon to the south, though perhaps a century later in inception, may prove to be another facet of the same, moving from the dry plains into the lush pastures of a separate highland mass.

The Highlands and the Lake region

At the same time there was occurring well to the west the expansion of Lwo communities in the northern parts of the old interlacustrine Bantu zone (illustrated in the previous section of this book) and along the eastern shores of Lake Victoria. This process, in districts good for cattle-keeping alongside cultivation, is often seen mistakenly as one of simple migration and conquest. It was equally a process of absorption of existing farming communities (some of whom satisfied their protein requirements by fishing in the lakes, swamps and rivers). Thus, successful settlement and population increase were accompanied by cultural adaptations which sometimes involved change of identity on a massive scale over a few generations. In this case of Lwo territorial expansion and assimilation, the principle of organization did not involve either age-sets or a developed form of chieftainship, but was based on a powerful sense of lineage and clan affiliation, with leading individuals whose names have been remembered. This was the key to settlement of the land and its fuller exploitation.

Similar in certain ways, yet not identical to that of the Lwo, was the impressive agricultural settlement of the Teso people east of Lake Kyoga, who thus created a broad wedge in the fertile savannas between the regions of northern and southern Lwo dominance. In doing so, the emerging Teso assimilated numbers of Lwo already settled in that district. The Teso pioneers, belonging linguistically to a very different branch of Nilotic known communally as Ateker, came from a pastoral tradition culturally akin to that of the Karimojong and Turkana who exploit the drier plains interspersed with grassy hills of what is now the northern Uganda-Kenya borderland. Here, as to the east, the economic and political affairs of the pastoral communities were organised through age systems with their own communal training and rituals. On this side the formation and initiation of age-sets did not involve circumcision, as was the practice of the highland peoples.

In outline therefore the history of the East African highlands and their surrounds over these several centuries is beginning to take shape. Much remains to be learned, but it is already plain enough that this history was one of continual change, on occasion revolutionary in its scale and effects, in which people's identities and ways of living were modified and often transformed. Among the factors was population increase, resulting from successful agriculture and exploitation of the pastures. In order to feed bigger numbers, new techniques of growing or obtaining food had to be devised. That meant new ways of organising society. There never was a static or 'traditional' African past.

The Swahili Harbour-Towns

Africa and the Wider World

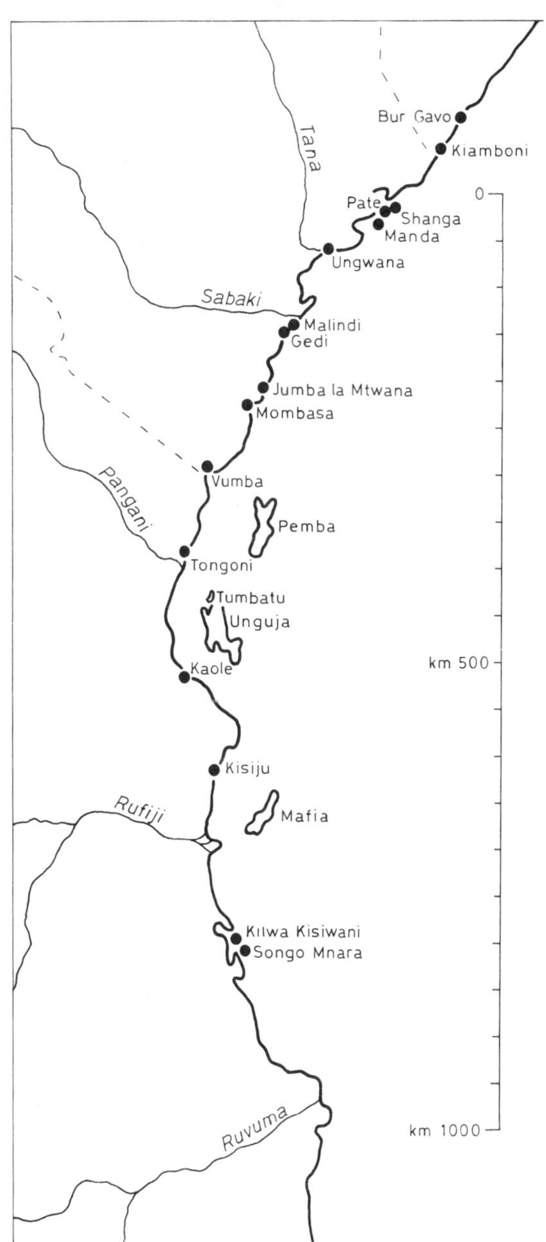

East Africa ends of course at the shore of the Indian Ocean. But the landsman who can see no further than the horizon, and who perceives the continent separate from the rest of the world, misses much of its culture and history – the interior history as well as that of the coast itself. To a sailor however the Ocean unites, as it has done for more than a thousand years, the African shores with the Red Sea, southern Arabia, the Persian Gulf and India. He knows the differences between all these countries, but equally the common threads which link them from one harbour to the next. For a harbour can never be entirely foreign; it must always possess a cosmopolitan touch, however slight, sufficient to welcome strangers and to tolerate their different customs, religions and speech. Often a lingua franca and broadly acknowledged rules of trading and behaviour are important mechanisms ensuring smooth relations between visitors and residents.

Thus the Swahili people of the coast and islands of what is now Tanzania and Kenya (with extensions into Mozambique, the Comores and Somalia), while decidedly African in their ancestry and culture, relate at the same time to a much wider world. At the superficial level one notices this in the coconut-palms fringing the shore and in the coastal cuisine with its preference for rice and spices, as well as fish naturally. Equally it is shown in the boats for fishing, for travel and for transport of goods, and especially in the designs of the larger dhows for distant voyages. Particularly important is Islam, whose practice and learning connects the Swahili people with those of many of the distant shores and harbours. To an up-country way of thinking, being Swahili and being Muslim can sometimes mean virtually the same thing. The reality of course is not so simple.

Swahili

This contact with the wider world, economic and intellectual at the same time, goes back twelve-hundred years, and has distinguished the Swahili (meaning literally the coast-dwellers) from their hinterland neighbours.

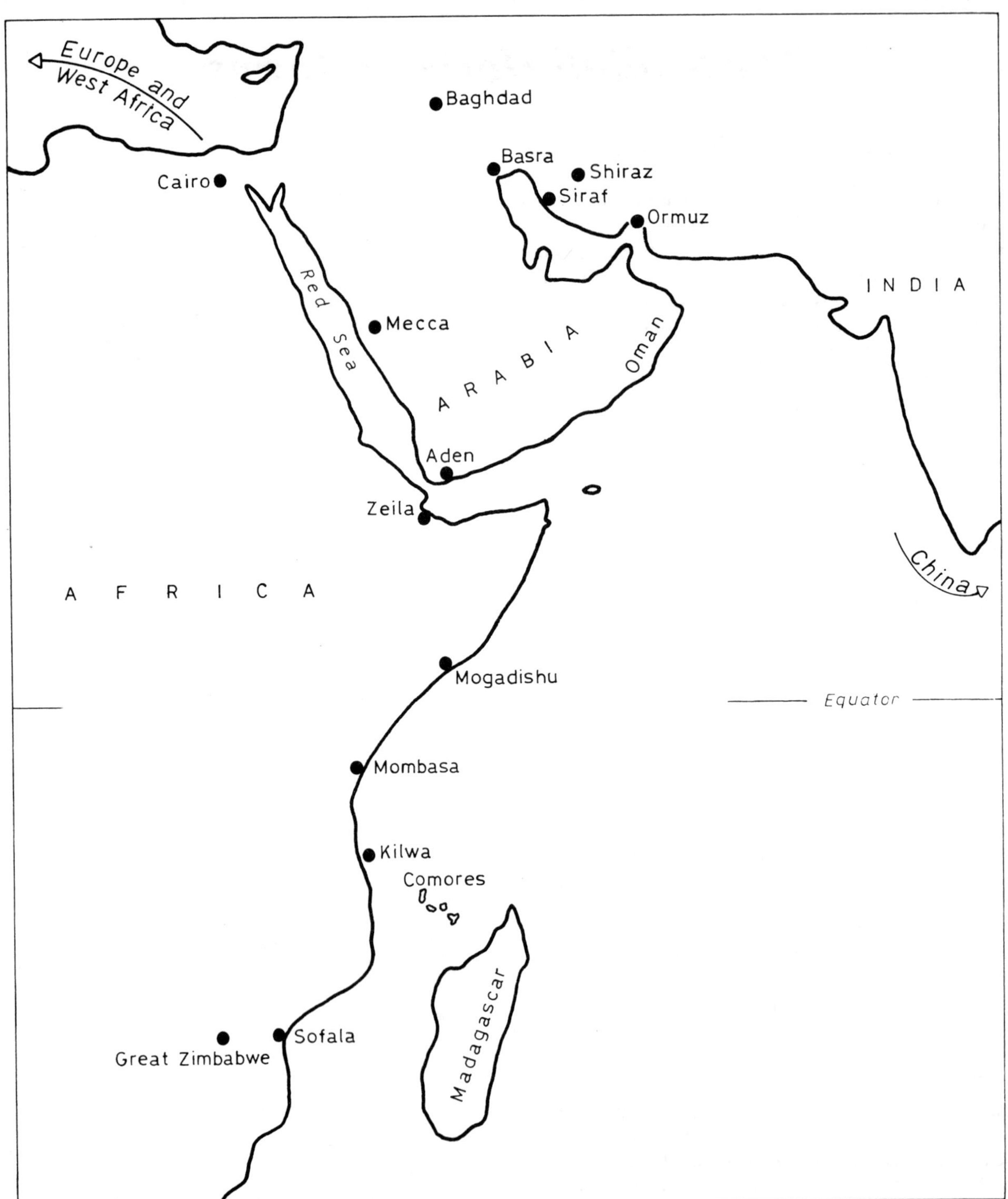
Europe and West Africa
Baghdad
Basra
Shiraz
Siraf
Ormuz
Cairo
INDIA
Red Sea
Mecca
ARABIA
Oman
Aden
Zeila
China
AFRICA
Mogadishu
Equator
Mombasa
Kilwa
Comores
Madagascar
Sofala
Great Zimbabwe

The harbour front of Kilwa Kisiwani, looking towards the fort known as Gereza

Stone tombs, 14th-century and later, now overlooked by coconut-palms, at the former roadstead-harbour of Kaole

Yet it is from the latter that the Swahili are derived, their social and economic organization being largely a coastal adaptation of that of the agricultural and pastoral communities on their landward side. The Swahili language belongs to the Bantu family, its structure, grammar and basic vocabulary all conforming with the north-eastern Bantu pattern. Because of this it has proved ideal as a lingua franca, expanding with remarkable rapidity among speakers of other Bantu languages at two widely separated historical periods.

The first expansion would have been in the 9th and 10th centuries AD parallel with the development of shipping and trade along the coast, and at the same time of connections with the Islamic lands and around the Indian Ocean generally. It was then that the Swahili language spread from its northern end (the Lamu archipelago and the present Somalia border of Kenya) southwards to the islands and emerging coastal harbours as far as southern Tanzania, the Comores and places in Mozambique.

This is not simply a deduction from the geographical distribution of Swahili dialects; it is corroborated archaeologically. There is a distinctive tradition of locally made pottery found on seaside and harbour sites in these countries, conveniently dated to this period by their being found together with rarer pieces of wheel-made glazed vessels originating in the Persian Gulf and other Islamic regions. Some of this early Swahili-style pottery was made inland, especially along the river basins behind the northern coast. The significance of these discoveries – in particular whether they indicate commercial exploitation for ivory and other products along the Rufiji, Pangani, Sabaki and Tana valleys at this early period – has not yet been adequately explored.

The Swahili language's second period of expansion occurred a thousand years later, with the development of regular and formal trade-routes penetrating the East African interior in the 19th century. It was then rapidly adopted as the lingua franca up-country as far as the great lakes and the upper Congo basin. From this base it has naturally become the national language of Tanzania and Kenya, but especially effectively in the former country. Even a hundred years ago a schoolboy at St Andrew's College, Kiungani on Zanzibar, could write:

> We are so many boys in this house, and of different tribes, Yaos, Makuas, Bondeis and Nyassas; but we all speak the Swahili language.
>
> Letter discovered by John Iliffe in USPG/UMCA archives, and quoted by Wilfred Whiteley in his *Swahili: the rise of a national language* (Methuen, London, 1969), p.57.

It is often pointed out that Swahili vocabulary contains a large number of words of Arabic derivation. That is correct; and it is easy to pick out many such words of non-Bantu origin (adapted though they have been by sound-shifts and Swahili prefixes). What is less well understood however is that the bulk of these borrowings are not ancient in (Ki)Swahili, but belong to the last two-hundred years or so (the period of the 'new' Arabs and the Zanzibari state). One important effect of this expanded vocabulary of recent centuries with its cultural and technical versatility has been to render Swahili viable as a written language in the modern world, first using the Arabic alphabet, later the Latin one. Earlier literacy on the East African coast had relied on the Arabic language.

The proper way of living

Although the coast people, those who speak the various dialects of (Ki)Swahili as their mother tongue, are known collectively by outsiders as (Wa)Swahili, they have not necessarily identified themselves in that way. Usually they prefer local names (for instance Bajuni in the far north) or those of clans or places of supposed origin (Shirazi among others). Many like to be known as *(wa)ungwana*, meaning something equivalent to 'free men', thus reflecting notions of class and ancestry. In some towns the connotation *ungwana* is more rarefied, alluding to certain ancient families whose leaders have been the quintessential representatives of this urban and civilised community. Swahili social history is an immensely fascinating subject but one too complex to attempt here. Suffice it to notice how these societies have perceived the urban, literate and Islamic qualities which, they feel, have distinguished themselves from the *shenzi* 'uncivilised' hinterland folk. Typically, a modern poet, Hasani bin Ismail of Kilwa Kivinje, after reciting his ballad about the famous witchcraft-eradicator and crime-detector nicknamed Nguvumali, felt he should remind his audience:

> Ninakaa mashambani — I live now in a country village
> Mjini nimezaliwa. — Yet a townsman was I born.
>
> *Swifa ya Nguvumali*, verse 393,
> translated and edited by Peter Lienhardt as
> *The Medicine Man* (Oxford, Clarendon Press, 1968).

Islam

The architecture and layout of the coastal towns, and not only of the mosques, are Islamic in the broad sense. But, despite popular thinking, they are not 'Arab'. Both in the styles and in the building techniques and materials, Swahili Islamic architecture is distinct from that of Arabia (just as Turkish and Indian and West African Islamic are all distinct and not to be described as 'Arab'). The misapprehension that the Swahili and their cultural history are Arab or 'half-Arab' is based on a shallow historical understanding. The claims of many Swahili families, for reasons of prestige within Muslim society, to a distant Arab origin have encouraged an exaggerated notion of Arab settlement of the coast in earlier centuries. The contacts and a variety of influences deriving from them are undeniable; yet the Swahili remain an East African people.

It is within both its local African and its broader Islamic context therefore that Swahili history has to be studied. Islam's universal appeal, its sects and divisions notwithstanding, brought the coast into a wider intellectual world. This cosmopolitan tendency went hand in hand with the development of commerce between diverse people around the Indian Ocean. It was in the first place for such commercial, not religious, reasons that the sea-routes were pioneered, techniques of efficient ocean-sailing mastered, harbours developed and the network maintained.

The old Swahili harbour-towns

These towns of the East African littoral flowered at their fairest in the 14th and 15th centuries. That was the time of the greatest stone-building activity and architectural diversity. New settlements, such as Songo Mnara on the island next to Kilwa, Gedi by Malindi and Jumba la Mtwana north of Mombasa, were laid out; while older ones, notably Shanga and Kilwa Kisiwani itself, were replanned. All these are now famous as ruins bearing witness both to their former greatness when local and international commerce were at their peak – with gold from the south being especially in demand – and equally to their decline and in some cases collapse in the 16th century.

The main factor in that eventual decline was the disruption of the old trade-routes and established commercial system resulting from the Portuguese rounding of the Cape of Good Hope and intervention in the Indian Ocean from 1498 onwards. Kilwa itself was acutely affected by the new shipping axis from Mozambique Island to Goa, together with Portuguese attempts to capture any gold reaching Sofala and the Zambezi mouth. If Portuguese

Ruins of 14th-century Swahili architecture: the mosque at Tongoni (showing mihrab and row of pillars to support roof, now collapsed), and rich houses at Gedi. Both sites were excavated in the 1950s: Tongoni by Neville Chittick for the Tanganyika Antiquities, Gedi by James Kirkman for the Kenya National Parks (now Museums).
A tomb at Gedi, bearing a stone inscription with the date of 1399 AD, is valuable for separating the 14th- from the 15th-century structures.

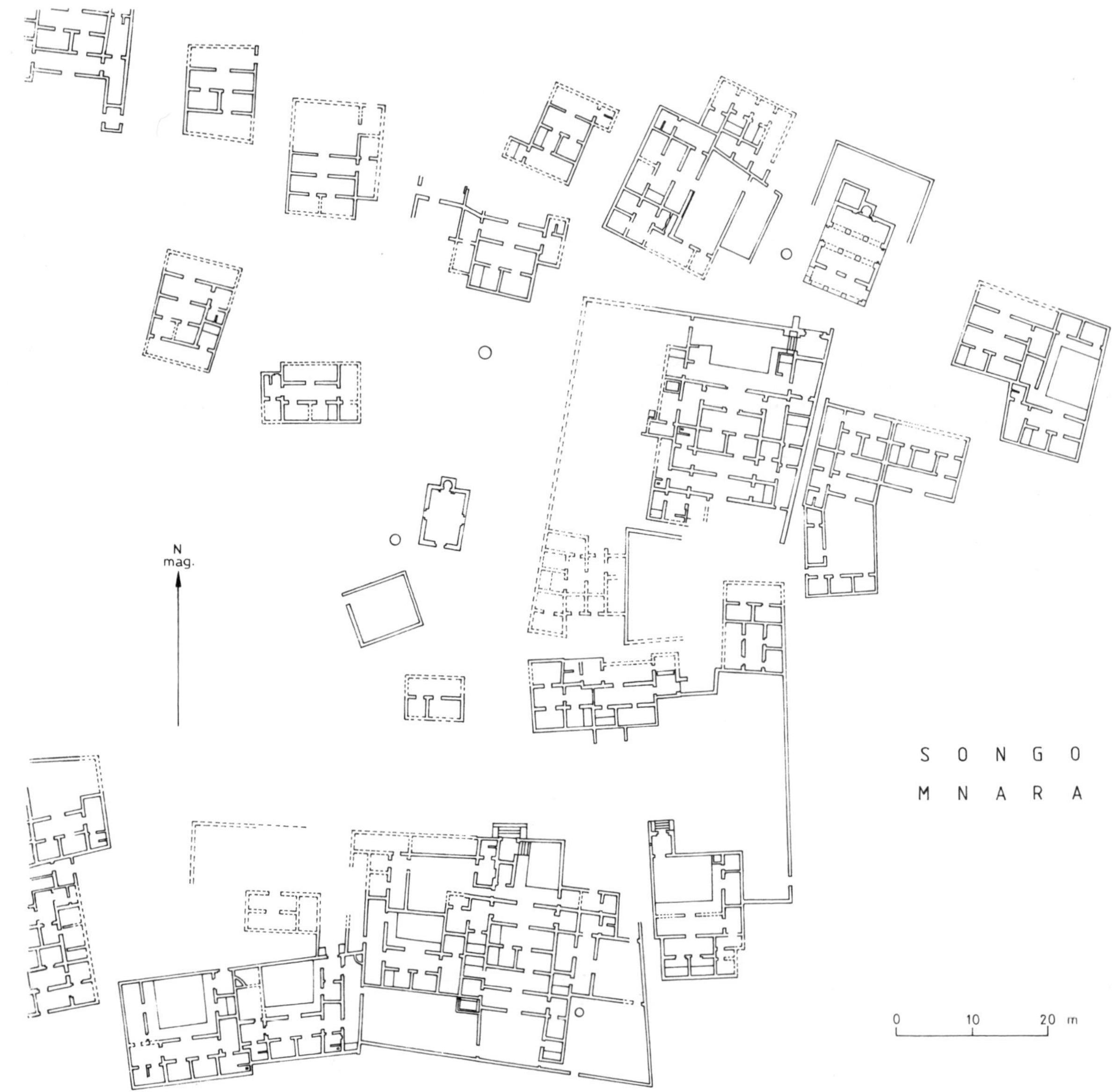

The stone buildings of the eastern part of the 14th-15th century town of Songo Mnara, on an island in the Kilwa group, as surveyed by Peter Garlake. (Certain of the buildings were reused and modified in the time of the revival of commercial activity in the 18th century.)
Most of the buildings were houses, the bigger ones containing numerous rooms and interior courtyards, in some instances stepped (photo opposite). The mosques are easily distinguished by the mihrab projections in the qibla wall facing Mecca, that is north in this part of the world. The rectangular enclosures on the north side of the northern mosque and south of the central mosque are graveyards. Other graves lie scattered in the open areas to west and east. The wells, for fresh water for domestic needs – and also for ablutions before entering the mosques – are drawn to scale as small circles; others exist outside the built-up area.

failed to suppress completely the Swahili route, it was effectively downgraded among the world's lanes of commerce. Another factor, real but perhaps exaggerated by some historians, for the decline of the Swahili towns was noted above, namely the encroachment of sections of pastoral Galla (or Oromo/Orma) into the northern coastal strip in the late 16th century. Several towns on the north mainland were abandoned from that time, through a combination of insecurity and economic strain.

Not all the harbours declined irreversibly however. The obvious exception is Mombasa. This was already an old town when the Portuguese arrived. In the 15th century it had overtaken Kilwa to become the largest on the coast. For within the Swahili coastline, Mombasa's position was more central; it was also better placed for serving the growing trade with Cambay (the Gujerat region) in India. From Mombasa a dhow, well rigged and manned, might attempt the return trip to Cambay on one monsoon more reliably than from Kilwa lying well to the south. If Mombasa declined somewhat in the early part of the Portuguese period of control – and it suffered a series of sackings at Portuguese hands – it flourished and expanded again in the latter part, that is the 17th century.

Later towns

In the 18th and 19th centuries, after the Portuguese had lost control of this coast, new international demands, for ivory and slaves especially, resulted in a second Swahili boom period. This occurred alongside a heightening of power politics in the Indian Ocean and its closer incorporation into the world economy. In this situation the Zanzibar state under its Omani rulers gradually extended control over the coastal towns from the 1770s onwards. But several of these maintained a measure of independence of direct Zanzibari control well into the 19th century as they naturally rose to the new economic challenge. Mombasa is once more the prime example. Some other towns which thrived in this period, notably Lamu, were old but hitherto rather unimportant. Others again were entirely new, for instance Bagamoyo on the mainland opposite Zanzibar; or Kilwa Kivinje, likewise founded on the mainland for the convenience of the upcountry caravans a short distance from old Kilwa (Kisiwani, 'on the island'). Somewhat later, in the mid-1860s, Dar es Salaam was founded by the sultan of Zanzibar, Sayyid Majid, as his own mainland town, his 'House of Peace', to rival Bagamoyo. Nowadays there is a popular idea of these towns as 'old': they are in fact the *new* Swahili towns, not to be confused with those of the early Swahili system of five-hundred and more years ago.

The 14th century and the world gold demand

That system, as mentioned, reached its apogee in the 14th century. Well documented at Kilwa with its stone mosques, houses and palaces, the relics of the period can be seen at numerous other sites on the coast and islands of Tanzania, Kenya and southmost Somalia. It is no coincidence that further south in the African interior, at Great Zimbabwe, the 14th century also saw the greatest concentration of population and building activity. There the architecture, the configuration of the settlement, the building materials and the construction techniques were

Manda: digging below water-level into the earliest occupation of the 9th-10th centuries, beside the later massive sea-walls.

Shanga: the post-holes of a succession of 9th-century wooden mosques below the remains of the 10th-11th-century stone mosque. (Photo, Mark Horton)

entirely different from those of the Swahili, the Shona cultural tradition of Zimbabwe evolving quite independently. But the reason behind it all – the local power and wealth which commissioned the buildings in effect – was essentially identical. This was the international demand for raw materials, and in particular the thirst for gold in the early 14th century – in the Islamic lands, in the Far East and especially in Europe – exerting unprecedented pressure to exploit all known and workable sources and to stimulate prospection beyond. A place which could control the mines and act as collecting and marketing point, as did Great Zimbabwe, or which could make itself the international transshipment port, as did Kilwa, found itself flourishing exceptionally during that half-century.

At this very period – the two generations preceding the Black Death, to keep it in world context – parallel developments occurred in the far west of Africa. Here the empire of Mali attained its greatest power and international fame since it exercised control over the most productive of the Guinea goldfields. With new ones being explored in Akanland at the same time, a vast web of trade-routes was coordinated. It connected with the trans-Saharan camel-caravans on a hitherto unequalled scale, paralleling the dhow traffic of the East coast of Africa and the Red Sea. Neither in West Africa nor on the eastern side was gold the only factor of course; but because of its intrinsic value internationally and the specific nature of its sources – much more specific than with ivory for instance, for elephants may roam while rocks stay fixed – gold has had a disproportionate impact on the directions of commerce and its intensity. Owing to the volatility of international demands, with sudden slumps succeeding unpredictable booms, the effects on the less developed sides of the trade networks can be destructive as well as constructive.

The rise of Swahilidom

If the first half of the 14th century was the most 'golden age' of the old Swahili, this maritime civilization with its international commercial connections did not arise then out of nothing. Its roots stretch back almost twice that age, to the beginning of the 9th century AD. That was the time of the opening of the Indian Ocean trading network. At first this commerce was oriented towards the Persian Gulf, the gateway to the Abbasid empire with its capital at Baghdad.

Several sites of this earliest period are known on the coast and islands of Kenya and Tanzania. The most important are in the Lamu archipelago – Manda (excavated by Neville Chittick) and Shanga (where Mark Horton has been digging since with exciting results). Here have been found, aside the ancient well, the foundations of a mosque dating about 800 AD, that is much earlier than had been expected for Islamic practice in East Africa. It was built – and rebuilt several times – of wood, until in the 10th century it was superseded by a stone mosque. That too underwent alterations and reconstructions. These discoveries lead some authorities to speculate whether Shanga – or Shanga and Manda and other sites in these islands together – may be Qanbalu, visited by al-Masudi in a ship from Oman in 916 AD. It had a Muslim ruling family, and had been founded at least a century previously. But others believe that Qanbalu was further south, on Pemba or the Comores. Its actual location, when confirmed, will do a lot for the understanding of East African and Indian Ocean history in this early Islamic period.

Exports from the land of the Zanj

Masudi reported the quality of East African ivory, noting ruefully the fierce international competition for this commodity more than a thousand years ago:

> The tusks usually go to Oman, and from there are sent to China and India. This is the chief trade route, and were it not so, ivory would be plentiful in Muslim lands.

Ambergris, derived from whales and used for perfumes, was another prized product of the African shores. Also in demand in rich Chinese households were leopard-skins, for saddles as well as rugs. Rhino-horn similarly had a Far Eastern market, in this case medicinal.

It was not just a trade in luxury items. Idrisi, writing somewhat later as far away as Sicily, heard of the production and export of East African iron. No less important was timber, especially mangrove-poles, needed by the construction industry at Oman, Siraf, Basra and other towns of treeless south-eastern Arabia and the Persian Gulf. In the 9th century 'Zanj' slaves from East Africa were taken in numbers, in particular to work the salt at Basra at the head of the Gulf and to drain the marshes of lower Iraq. After the slave revolt of the late 9th century this particular trade declined very sharply (slave exports from East Africa remaining slight for another nine centuries).

By 'Zanj' was meant black people, but in particular East Africans. 'Zanzibar' (or occasionally Zangistan in Persian or Hindi texts) was the 'land of the Zanj', the whole Swahili coast. Only in time did the name become associated specifically with the island which is properly called Unguja.

'The meadows of gold' and copper from the south

From the southern African interior came copper as well as the gold of Zimbabwe and the Limpopo bend. These were carried to the south Mozambique coast – 'the land of Sofala which produces gold and many other wonderful things' in Masudi's phrase – and thence channelled through the East African harbours into the international commercial network. For the economic stimulus generated by the Abbasids and their gold dinars was felt far beyond the bounds of their formal Islamic empire. It is reflected in the Far East, in western Europe and across the Sahara in Far-West Africa, the principal gold-producing region of the continent. In Zimbabwe the archaeological evidence, even from the mines themselves, corroborates Masudi's information that it was at this very time that gold began to be exploited there and to bring the region into the international scene.

Madagascar and the Indonesian connection

Beyond Qanbalu and in the region of Sofala the land of the Zanj was thought to approach the islands of the Waqwaq. There were in those days both eastern and western 'Waqwaq' – as Arab sailors and writers knew them – the former inhabiting the Malayo-Indonesian region, the latter settling in Madagascar. Some doubtless visited the African shores opposite.

'The Book of the Wonders of India' – which is a 10th-century collection of sailors' tales and other stories on the borderland between fact and fiction – tells of a Waqwaq fleet attacking Qanbalu in the year 945/6 AD. They 'came in a thousand ships', it is said; nevertheless, Qanbalu's island defences held firm. This raid was occasioned by competition for the control of the commerce of this region into which Arab shipping had been infiltrating in the previous century. The cementing of the Swahili alliance, helped by gradual Islamization of the harbour-towns, and not only of Qanbalu, was an essential element in this successful penetration. The orientation of East Africa from that time remained towards the northerly rim of the Indian Ocean and the mainstream of Old World civilization and commerce, not towards the more peripheral and fragmenting sphere of the Waqwaq.

The Waqwaq legacy

The recognition of the cultural and linguistic relationship of the two divisions of the Waqwaq led some Arab geographers to surmise that the Indian Ocean was merely a large lake, with southern Africa curving to join with the East Indies. Masudi himself did not concur with this notion, having spoken with an Arab mariner who had sailed far enough south to refute it, or so he claimed. (Others had gone that far south but had not shared this one's miraculous luck in getting back against the currents to report.) Yet Masudi was no less conscious of the cross-oceanic connections of these Waqwaq during and preceding this period of Arab navigational expansion.

After the 10th century the power of the Waqwaq and the range of their sailing exploits declined. The settlers of Madagascar were left to develop independently of their Indonesian cousins; later immigrants to the Great Island came no longer from Asia but from Africa. (Eventually it became known as Madagascar, which is a corrupt form of the name Mogadishu, through some strange confusion which has been attributed to Marco Polo, the 13th-century Venetian traveller, or rather to his careless readers.)

That notwithstanding, the old Indonesian factor in the Indian Ocean has been an important one culturally and economically. In particular it is to that period, a full thousand years ago, that we should trace the introduction of bananas to Africa, on whose eastern side they have been developed as a staple food for wetter regions and at the same time diversified more than anywhere else in the world, indeed thoroughly Africanised.

West and East

In the north-westerly quarter of the Ocean the importance of Baghdad and the Persian Gulf routes was by 1000 AD declining relatively, whereas traffic in the Red Sea leading to Egypt was developing rapidly. Thus the city of

Minuscule silver coin of about 1000 AD, from Fatimid mint in Sicily, found at Manda. As preserved, it measures one centimetre. Such coins illustrate the new direction of trade through the Red Sea and Egypt, linking the Indian Ocean with the Mediterranean.

Equally small are the locally made silver coins discovered on Pemba. This hoard comprises over two thousand of which five (both sides) are shown (photo, Mark Horton). They are dated to the late 11th century, because of a few Fatimid gold dinars in the same purse (the newest one struck in 1066 AD). These silver coins of early Swahili rulers include some bearing the name of Ali bin al-Hasan, more frequently found on the not dissimilar copper coins found in vast numbers at Mafia and Kilwa *(p.78-9)**. This is presumably the same Ali bin al-Hasan mentioned in the* Kilwa Chronicle *as the founder of that city and sultanate.*

The change in the metal used in the Swahili mints towards the end of the 11th century reflects a preference, doubtless dictated by economic considerations, for importing and working copper obtained from the southern African interior (along the gold and ivory routes) and against remelting silver (perhaps already in the form of coin) from Muslim and eastern countries.

Cairo came to assert a pivotal role between the trade of the Indian Ocean, including East Africa, and that of the Mediterranean, linking with the developing European as well as North African and Byzantine markets. Increased demands for East African ivory in the 11th century are reflected by silver and occasional gold coins from Fatimid Egypt found at places on the Swahili coast and islands (and the beginnings of local coinages, first in silver and then in copper, the latter metal obtained from the southern African trade).

This Egyptian direction was not the sole one. The commerce between East Africa and India also increased, and continued doing so until the 16th century (when the Portuguese intervened). So did that with China, although this was mostly indirect. Chinese celadon and porcelain – whose broken pieces are common on old Swahili town sites, where these fine bowls had been used to decorate mosques, tombs and houses among other purposes – were transshipped at one or more intermediate ports (such as Malacca, Cambay, Oman and Aden). African ivory conversely reached China by stages.

Only very rarely did actual Chinese ships visit Africa. One famous exception was about 1420 AD, an occasion used by the Sultan of Malindi – one of the principal Swahili states of the time, which probably combined the fair city and palace of Gedi – to send a distinctive gift to the Emperor of China. This 'celestial animal', as it was recognised at the other end, has been immortalised on Chinese silk (over).

Chinese porcelain, especially celadon and blue-on-white, can be dated quite precisely by changes in fashion. When found in an archaeological deposit or in the ruins of a Swahili building, it provides a minimum dating. An individual vessel may of course have been preserved as a prized possession for a long time before being accidentally broken and its pieces (sherds) discarded. But where one finds several such imported vessels or sherds of them, one can date with fair confidence from them or from the latest one in the assemblage.
The practice of fixing Chinese bowls into the plaster of Swahili masonry for decorative effect is especially useful for dating buildings including mosques and tombs.

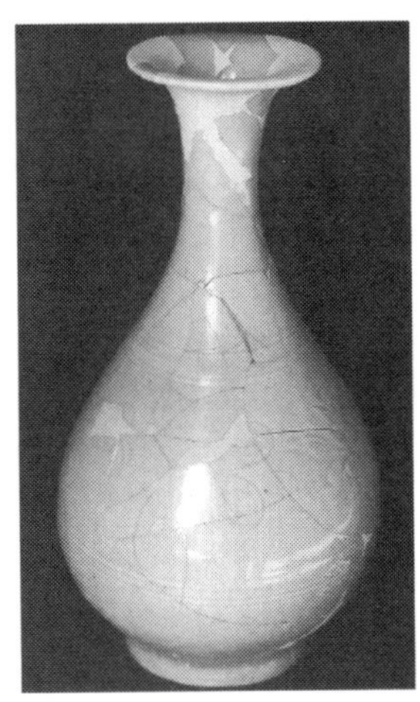

This glazed porcelain flask, made in China in Yuan times about 1300 AD, was found in some fifty pieces while excavating a well in the ruins of Husuni Kubwa palace at Kilwa. Its colour is powder-blue, with incised floreate decoration below the glaze; its height 27 cm.

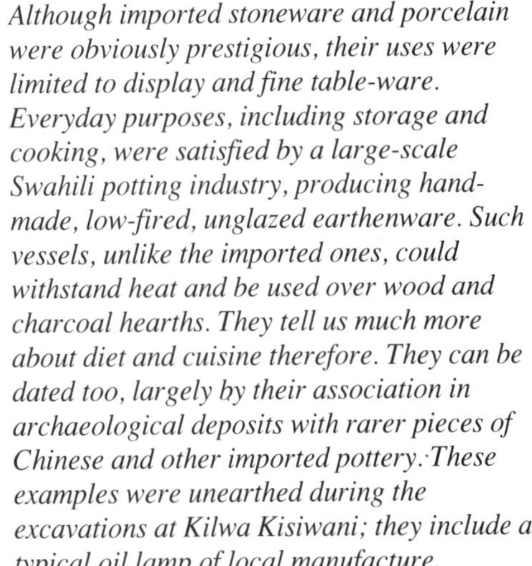

Although imported stoneware and porcelain were obviously prestigious, their uses were limited to display and fine table-ware. Everyday purposes, including storage and cooking, were satisfied by a large-scale Swahili potting industry, producing hand-made, low-fired, unglazed earthenware. Such vessels, unlike the imported ones, could withstand heat and be used over wood and charcoal hearths. They tell us much more about diet and cuisine therefore. They can be dated too, largely by their association in archaeological deposits with rarer pieces of Chinese and other imported pottery. These examples were unearthed during the excavations at Kilwa Kisiwani; they include a typical oil lamp of local manufacture.

There seems to have been a sudden fashion for shipping giraffes to the Chinese court and imperial menagerie in the early 15th century. They were thought to resemble mythical unicorns. This particular giraffe made a 'stop-over' in Bengal, whose Muslim ruler took the credit for presenting it to the Emperor of China.

Kilwa

City and port

Lying towards the southerly end of the old Swahili settlements, Kilwa was from the 12th to 14th centuries the most important. It controlled the trade with the Mozambique Channel and Sofala, including high-quality ivory and the gold of Zimbabwe.

Like Manda and Shanga well to the north, Kilwa is situated on an island, one of a small archipelago in a sunken estuary. The crossing from the mainland to Kilwa Kisiwani takes under half-an-hour unless wind and tide are contrary. The situation provides not only security but also an excellent sheltered harbour for sailing craft of all sizes. Settlement and commercial activity began here as

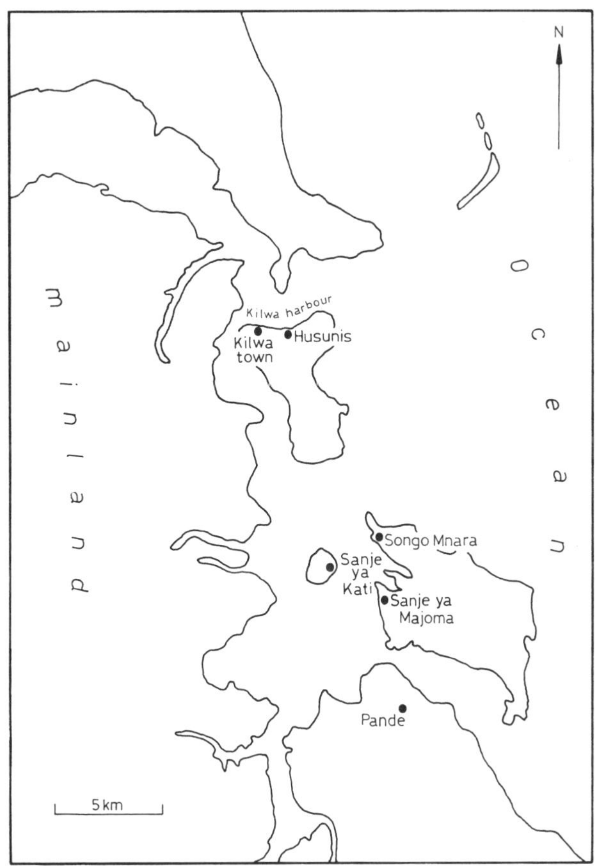

The Kilwa archipelago

early as the 9th century, the same period as at Shanga and Manda. For two or three centuries those northerly harbours remained more prosperous. But by 1100 AD Kilwa and the southern Swahili were coming into their own.

For part of this formative period the larger offshore island of Mafia, a little to the north, may have been as important as Kilwa itself. The early history of Kilwa and its sultanate, recorded below, may combine the memories of the two islands where a single ruling house emerged.

The story of the Great Mosque

The focal point of a Swahili town is the great mosque, that where the communal Friday prayers are conducted. Usually the finest building, it is, on some deserted sites, the only ruin to survive above ground. Thus the history of the Friday mosque is the key to that of the town.

It is not yet known for certain whether the early Muslim community at Kilwa made do with a wooden mosque, as has been revealed at Shanga. But by the late 11th century Kilwa could boast a stone mosque. It was modest in size; its style typical of the coast. A flat coral-concrete roof was laid over mangrove-rafters, themselves supported by the walls and internal rows of pillars. If left to decay, such roofs eventually collapsed. The roofless shell of this first mosque is seen at the lower left of the air-photograph. On the plan it is shown at the top (north). The holes for the cut rafters which supported the roof are visible on the outside at ceiling level (photos, p.72).

The unprecedented boom about 1300, fuelled by renewed international gold demands, is reflected at Kilwa in massive and ornate building activities. The grand palace of Husuni Kubwa (described below) did much to set this monumental trend. At the same time the Great Mosque was increased to over four times its original capacity, by means of an arched, domed and barrel-vaulted extension, most of which – after some 15th-century reconstruction – stands intact (as seen in the centre of the air-photograph).

Kilwa: the Great Mosque (after Garlake and Chittick). This and other ruins at Kilwa were excavated in the early 1960s by Neville Chittick for the Tanganyika Antiquities and the British Institute. The finds are deposited in the National Museum in Dar es Salaam.

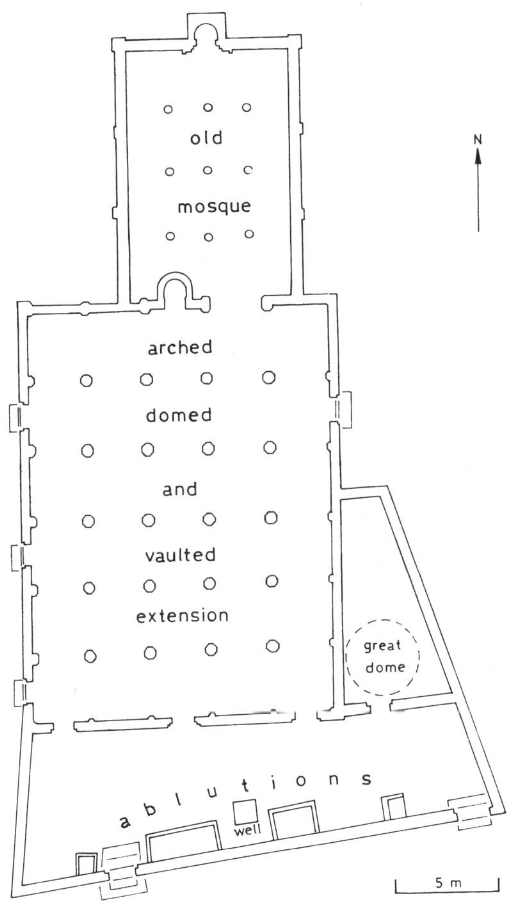

Architecture and masonry

However the great south-eastern dome (under which, it is said, the sultan himself was wont to pray) has fallen. In fact the whole structure required attention and repair from time to time. There is a touching story, recorded in the 'Kilwa Chronicle', of the mosque's collapse about 1350 or so, and its restoration half-a-century later. In the meantime 'the people prayed under shelters and tents'. This is doubtless exaggeration (and there is a problem in following the chronicler's dating): almost certainly the mosque remained partly in use, if not in the best repair, through the depressed period. But this could be an oblique acknowledgement of the decimating impact of the Black Death which in the years around 1350 was carried by trading vessels to most of the ports of the Old World. It seems unlikely that Kilwa and other Swahili towns in the international network would have escaped this scourge. In which case the population of Kilwa may for a couple of generations have been so reduced as to feel neither the need nor the energy to worry about the collapse of part of this great mosque.

Whatever the real background to this episode, the allusion in the Chronicle to the solid cut-stone pillars which defeated the ingenuity of later masons is not invention: they were left lying alongside the mosque –where they remain to this day – demanding an explanation. (See photos, p.72-3.)

In the time of Sultan Sulaiman ibn al-Malik al-Adil, historians say that the Friday mosque, which had collapsed in the reign of Abu al-Mawahib, was restored. The prime mover was Sayyid Hajj Rush, son of Sultan Husain. He asked Sultan Sulaiman permission to rebuild it at his own expense. Permission was not given, but the sovereign gave him a thousand mithkals of gold and said: 'Rebuild the mosque with this money.' And Sayyid Hajj Rush meditated the matter and said to himself: 'Unless I take this money, permission to rebuild the mosque will be refused. Thus it is best to accept the money, but I shall rebuild it at my own expense.' So he took the money, and rebuilt it at his own expense until it was complete. When Sultan Sulaiman died, Hajj Rush returned the money to his heirs.

It was done thus under God's guidance. When the mosque was being restored, they lacked wood to rebuild the pillars. For the original pillars were of cut stone, and there were now no masons who could reassemble them as they were previously. This had perplexed them and had prevented the restoration. But by Divine Providence a great tree was cast up on shore, of exactly the right length, the tree being complete with its root and branches. They made pillars for the front part of the mosque from the trunk, and there were seven pillars in all. From the branches they made rafters and crossbeams for the front part and the two wings. At the back they built domes in imitation of the dome of Abu al-Mawahib as aforesaid.

The author has himself seen the man who saw the tree as mentioned, and he is Sultan Muhammad ibn Sultan al-Husain ibn Sultan Sulaiman. The latter (Sulaiman) gave the order for the rebuilding of the mosque, while the first-named ordered the writing of this history. God knows all truth.

The northern, original, part of the Great Mosque: the three rows of post-holes inside for wooden pillars to support the roof; and the outer wall with slots for the roofing rafters.

Pillars of piety and prestige

Nicely illustrated here are notions of piety and proper Islamic observance in the 15th century – or at least in the eyes of those who retold the tale afterwards. More subtly it betrays the tradition of fierce competition for prestige within Swahili society. In this instance Sayyid Rush, who had already distinguished himself by performing the pilgrimage to Mecca, managed to assert his moral superiority over his kinsmen, even the sultan and his heirs.

In recalling this rebuilding of the mosque, the chronicler's understanding of technical detail failed to match his religious faith, while his obsession with the number *seven* defies mathematical and architectural sense. One may feel sceptical too about wooden pillars being fashioned to hold the concrete roof of a stone building. But if we take him at his word that they were used in reconstructing the 'front part' of the mosque, that is the ancient flat-roofed one at the north – which required *nine* pillars, in three rows of three – the evidence from Chittick's excavations bears him out. A comparable example is at Kaole, a small town of similar date near Bagamoyo, in the ruins of whose southern mosque the stone sockets to hold the bases of wooden pillars remain visible in the floor.

But, for the great domed extension of Kilwa's Friday mosque – where the solid pillars had proved unsatisfactory – the masons' eventual solution was to construct substitutes of composite stone blocks (as seen in the interior photograph). These did the trick – this unique piece of domed and barrel-vaulted roofing surviving from the 14th or early 15th century to the late 20th.

The west wall of the Great Mosque and the domed and arched extension supported on rows of octagonal pillars made of composite stone. Note the solid cut-stone pillars lying discarded outside the mosque.

Kilwa: the small domed mosque, built in three aisles each of three bays, roofed by alternating domes and barrel-vaults, the central dome supported by a square of four stone pillars. Inset Chinese bowls date this mosque to the 15th century.

Excavating the 'great house' adjoining the south side of the Great Mosque. Only the foundations of the walls remain.

Private and public worship

Like other Swahili towns of the 14th and 15th centuries, Kilwa was adorned with several smaller stone mosques. These are believed to have belonged to particular communities or prominent families, or served the various quarters of the town for daily prayer and devotion. In certain instances the masons and their patrons used the opportunity to repeat in miniature stylistic features of the domed Friday mosque. The event of the week however was attendance at the latter, graced by the presence of the ruler.

At this period it seems that the main Swahili Muslim communities, the rulers and commoners alike, were 'orthodox' Sunni following the Shaf'i school. But there are suggestions of Shi'i elements or parties in certain towns, notably Malindi and possibly Kilwa too. Nevertheless, the situation seems to have simplified from that of the 9th to llth centuries when there are indications of several heterodox Muslim communities at different times and places along the East African coast.

Dwellings for rich and poor

The 'great house' – whose excavated ruins appear on the air-photograph behind the domed mosque – dates for the most part about 1400, perhaps contemporary with the mosque's restoration. The masonry techniques were no different from those used for the mosques and palaces, both here at Kilwa and elsewhere along the coast. The basic structure was of coral-rag cemented in lime-mortar, the surfaces being smoothed and finally plastered. All these materials – as well as the fine cut-stonework for doorways, arches and lamp-niches – were local. They were prepared from coral by a range of techniques most of which have been maintained to this day by Swahili craftsmen. Cut-stone needs to be worked while the coral, quarried from the reef at lowest tides, is still wet and soft. Plaster and mortar are obtained by burning of coral.

Unlike the mosques and graves, the deserted houses have been robbed of much of their stone for re-use in later centuries. Often only the foundations, or merely the robber trenches, remain. But archaeologists, if excavating and recording diligently, can reconstruct from these.

Only the richer class could have afforded stone-built houses. Most of the townspeople, at Kilwa and the other Swahili settlements of the 14th and 15th centuries, built themselves houses in the coastal tradition of wood, earth and thatch. These materials need constant repair, and such houses would have been rebuilt every ten years or so and have thus contributed to the accumulation of occupation material which reveals the former town site. To conform with the orientation needs of a town with its streets and harbour-front, these houses of wood and earth would have been rectangular, as were those of stone. Being less spectacular than the stone remains, they have been given scant attention till now. It is hoped that new archaeological research will rectify this bias and allow a more balanced and realistic picture of these harbour-towns and their communities to emerge.

Kilwa described and remembered

Paradise Lost

In time Kilwa was eclipsed by Mombasa for economic reasons already explained. When Portuguese ships reached East Africa (following Vasco da Gama's voyage of 1498-99), Kilwa was still impressive, Mombasa more so. Yet the former's fame persisted as it declined further. It figured on the maps printed in Europe in the 16th and 17th centuries, so that the English poet John Milton was able to recall 'Quiloa', Malindi and Sofala among the fabled cities of this distant clime, thinking in error it to be the biblical Ophir of the tenth century BC. The gold-mining of Zimbabwe and the international commercial connections had already a long history, but were not that old!

King Solomon's mines were *not* here. This misconception, perpetuated to the present day by southern African pseudo-historical writing, did not begin with Rider Haggard's 19th-century fiction. Haggard, like Milton before him, derived it from romantic Portuguese writers of the 16th century, who felt the need to explain the new discoveries in the Indian Ocean by relation to existing knowledge, in this case the Old Testament history of the kings of Israel.

Perhaps they were encouraged to seek a link of this sort on noticing that the royal house of Kilwa had given its sons, in typical Islamic fashion, the best biblical-koranic kingly names, Talut, Daud and Sulaiman – Saul, David and Solomon.

Kilwa as somewhat fancifully depicted in a print of 1588.
The island measures in fact about five kilometres by three, and the ancient town covered a smaller proportion of it than shown. The ships too are enormously exaggerated.
Nevertheless, the shape of the island and that of its harbour on the protected north side (foreground) are quite faithfully reproduced. Songo Mnara appears on the horizon.

This map of East Africa (reproduced by kind permission of the British Library) was poached from Portugal and published in Amsterdam in 1596. (It was thought to contain valuable intelligence about 'the Indies' where the Dutch were beginning to challenge the Portuguese.) Unreliably informed about the interior, the cartographer's coastal detail is passable, albeit with exaggeration of estuaries, including that of Kilwa. Both the town and the kingdom are clearly marked Quiloa.

Vasco da Gama

The available Portuguese descriptions of Kilwa at that period moreover are second-hand and sloppy on detail. That relating to da Gama's visit in 1502 (during his second voyage to the Indian Ocean) gives an impression of a tightly built town. It is not strictly an eye-witness account, the author, Gaspar Correa, obtaining his information and writing his book much later. The description of the town, its buildings and their heights may be influenced by stereotyped pictures of newly discovered parts of the world. Correa's population estimate is much higher than others hazarded for the town of Kilwa at that period.

> The city is large and is of good buildings of stone and mortar with terraces, and the houses have much woodwork. The city comes down to the shore, and is entirely surrounded by a wall and towers, within which there may be 12,000 inhabitants. The country all round is very luxuriant with many trees and gardens of all sorts of vegetables, citrons, lemons, and the best sweet oranges that were ever seen, sugar-canes, figs, pomegranates, and a great abundance of flocks, especially sheep, which have fat in the tail, which is almost the size of the body, and very savoury. The streets of the city are very narrow, as the houses are very high, of three and four storeys, and one can run along the tops of them upon the terraces, as the houses are very close together. In the port there were many ships.
>
> The translation from Correa's *Lendas da India* is that of E.J. Stanley (for the Hakluyt Society, 1869, reproduced in Freeman-Grenville, 1962, p.66).

Fortunately, there are other written sources relating to this and previous times at Kilwa. They too have imperfections, but of different sorts.

The Kilwa Chronicle

'The Book of the Consolation of the History of Kilwa' is essentially an oral-historical composition, a version of which was about 1550 AD committed to paper, in the Arabic language, at the insistence of the reigning sultan. The scholar to whom this task of compilation was assigned tried unsuccessfully to excuse himself, pleading 'excessive cares and troublesome humours'. He remained apologetic about its content, 'incorporating unique material and strange designs in the manner of the loaded Ark. When I gave it to a critic to read, it drove him to talk of his sorrows.' He may have attached his name to the manuscript, but that page has been lost. He tells us however that he was born in 1499 – on 13th of May, to be precise – an incidental point which helps him to fix the date of the first arrival of 'Franks' (Portuguese) in East Africa under 'Al-Mirati' (Vasco da Gama). Here he interjects 'God curse it!', a mild way of acknowledging that with Christian European shipping invading the Indian Ocean, the world would never be the same again.

The story, from the foundation of Kilwa to his own time, was planned in ten chapters. Only seven were properly completed, and have survived in a late manuscript copy dated 1867. (This was obtained by Sayyid Barghash, Sultan of Zanzibar, in whose domain Kilwa was then included; he presented it in 1872 to Dr John Kirk, the British consul, who passed it to the British Museum.) An alternative version, which is useful for comparison and for understanding obscure passages, had been abridged and published in Portuguese in 1552 (in João de Barros' book 'Decadas da Asia').

On many points the Chronicle complements the archaeological findings and illustrates the architectural history of Kilwa. By naming each sultan in succession and briefly describing his reign – some gaps and muddles notwithstanding – it is invaluable for the ordering of the numerous copper coins found at Kilwa and Mafia, bearing the names of several of them. From those in turn, as well as from the Chinese and other imported ceramics, the buildings and architectural sequence are dated.

Myth and history

As with other histories, the first chapter, reproduced here, may be regarded as mythical. Even the devout author could barely disguise his scepticism. (He doubtless knew that the legendary omen of a rat observed gnawing a hole in the city wall had been told of other times and places.) Similarly, most modern historians regard the claim of origin in Shiraz in Persia as exaggeration if not outright invention. Yet historical texts of this sort require subtle treatment; and as a 'foundation charter' the story reflects the way in which elements of coastal Muslim society have perceived themselves. It also illustrates Kilwa's historical connection with Pemba and the northern Swahili coast (including both Shanga and Manda apparently) expressed metaphorically as sons of the same father.

Ali bin al-Hasan, the one said to have landed at Kilwa, was nevertheless a real person. Whether actually an immigrant or not, he was the ruler of both Kilwa and Mafia where large numbers of his copper coins have been found. He was remembered as 'Nguo Nyingi', having supposedly bought Kilwa island for reams of coloured cloth. The recent discovery of his name among the silver coins of Pemba may suggest a broader sphere of influence around 1050 AD or so.

That happens to be the dating, some four centuries after the Prophet, mentioned in the version of the Chronicle, now lost, which de Barros in the 16th century consulted in the Lisbon archives. Another anecdote recorded there, but later forgotten or suppressed, tells of this Ali's parentage, being born to a royal Persian father, named for good measure as Hasan or Husain, by an Abyssinian slave woman. This is a clichéd device to explain how the progeny, that is the ruling house of Kilwa till the 16th century, was noble, Muslim and African in complexion at the same time.

Why 'from Shiraz in the land of the Persians'?

The numerous coins of Ali bin al-Hasan found on the southerly Swahili islands are inspired, as seen, by the example of Fatimid Egypt; clearly it was the development of the commercial link between the Red and Mediterranean Seas which set the economic context for the age of this Ali and his immediate successors at Mafia and Kilwa, and of his confederates or rivals on Unguja and Pemba. But no-one has ever suggested that he came from a Red Sea port or from Cairo. The traditions of the Swahili, including this partisan version known as the 'Kilwa Chronicle', insist that on the contrary he 'came from Shiraz' in Persia of all places. Whatever his real ancestry, local or more distant, he was the founder of the dynasty remembered as 'Shirazi' which ruled Kilwa for the next two centuries. More than that, many of his and

THE KILWA CHRONICLE: CHAPTER I

The first man to come to Kilwa and found it, and his descent from the Persian kings of the land of Shiraz.

Historians have said, amongst their assertions, that the first man to come to Kilwa came in the following way. There arrived a ship in which there were people who claimed to have come from Shiraz in the land of the Persians. It is said there were seven ships: the first stopped at Mandakha (Manda kuu?); the second at Shaugu (Shanga?); the third at a town called Yanbu; the fourth at Mombasa; the fifth at the Green Island (Pemba); the sixth at Kilwa; and the seventh at Hanzuan (in the Comores). They say that the masters of these first six ships were brothers, and that the one who went to the town of Hanzuan was their father. God alone knows all truth.

I understand from a person interested in history, and one whom I trust, that the reason for their leaving Shiraz in Persia was that their sultan one day dreamed a dream. He was called Hasan : he was the father of these six men and the seventh of those who left. In his dream he saw a rat with an iron snout gnawing holes in the town wall. He interpreted the dream as a prophecy of the ruin of their country. When he had made certain that his interpretation of the dream was correct, he told his sons. He convinced them that their land would not escape destruction...

The passages from the Kilwa Chronicle reproduced in this chapter are based on the translation by G.S.P. Freeman-Grenville, *The East African Coast: select documents* (Oxford U.P., 1962), p.35f, simplified or paraphrased where appropriate.
The photocopy of a page of the Arabic manuscript has been supplied by the British Library and is reproduced here by permission.

Copper coins of Kilwa and Mafia (diameters 2 cm or so), with rhyming couplets:

obverse	reverse
The majestic sultan	*In the name of God*
Ali bin al-Hasan	*the compassionate, the merciful*

The date of Ali bin al-Hasan (the founder of Kilwa, according to the Chronicle of that town) has been variously estimated between 950 and 1200 A.D. It now seems he reigned around 1070, since his name occurs on some of the small silver coins (p.67) in the hoard at Mtambwe Mkuu on Pemba.

The glazed jar, in which over 500 of these copper coins, all of Ali bin al-Hasan, were found at Kisimani Mafia (by Chittick, while excavating outside a mosque wall), is of a type of 'sgraffiato' ware which was traded extensively in the western Indian Ocean in the 11th century.

his successors' subjects, in fact large sections of the Swahili people, chose to associate themselves with this clan name 'Shirazi', representing themselves therefore as his nominal descendants.

The explanation of this Shirazi legend has long exercised scholars of coastal history. In recent years most have moved away from the simplistic notion of direct migration from Persia and from a literal acceptance of the story of the seven ships. It has been suggested that that was already an anachronism in Ali bin al-Hasan's own time, in fact an attempt to accommodate memories of the older cultural and commercial connections between the Swahili coast and the Persian Gulf – and especially Siraf, the port of Shiraz – of the Manda-Shanga-Qanbalu period two centuries beforehand. In this way Ali bin al-Hasan and his associates (or dubious brothers) who began exploiting this region on a new scale could still lay claim to its most ancient Islamic tradition. Here indeed may be part of the answer. But new evidence from Unguja (that is Zanzibar island together with its offshore isle of Tumbatu) indicates a more specific link with Siraf and Shiraz in the late 11th century.

This evidence is artistic and epigraphic, and not all of it is new. At Kizimkazi, at the southern end of Unguja, is a mosque whose mihrab bears a celebrated inscription including the date of 500 H (1107 AD) carved in stone in the Kufic style of Arabic. A second such Kufic inscription, perhaps by the same hand, was discovered in 1989

A piece (44 cm long) of the Tumbatu inscription (photo, Mark Horton). The Kufic style of script, of the Siraf-Shirazi school, should date it about 1100 AD. It was carved locally, whether on Tumbatu itself or on the larger island of Unguja, from porites coral.

during Dr Mark Horton's excavations of a ruined mosque on Tumbatu. This particular construction is of later date, but the inscription, and probably the whole mihrab in which it had been set, must have been carried there from an older, presumably redundant, mosque in the district, built in the late 11th or early 12th century. Being cut from porites coral, both these inscriptions were indubitably carved locally. But their Kufic – or Shirazi – style is so distinctive that one can only conclude that the craftsman had done his schooling and apprenticeship in one of the workshops of Siraf if not of Shiraz itself. A similar inspiration can be seen in the calligraphy on the coins of Ali bin al-Hasan, illustrated above.

It was therefore from the Persian Gulf that Ali bin al-Hasan and his company derived much of their particular brand of Islamic learning and literacy, and it is this 'Shirazi' connection for which they preferred to be remembered. But on a less sentimental plane, one must recognise the new economic horizons which made this possible in the mid-to-late 11th century, namely the increased commercial activity in the western Indian Ocean whose main axis ironically bypassed the Persian Gulf by focussing more on the Red Sea and Egypt. Without this, Ali bin al-Hasan would never have left his name by minting coins or being mentioned in the history books – from the 'Kilwa Chronicle' to this one.

Some two centuries later Kilwa, under the new Abu al-Mawahib dynasty, achieved yet greater fame internationally. On one occasion early in the 14th century the internal sources, notably the Chronicle but also the inscriptions carved in stone and those cast on the coins, bear correlation with an independent source. It is not much of a description; it is more like a traveller's vague memory, patently confused on certain details, yet revealing on the general situation.

Ibn Battuta's Africa:

'The Nile descends from Mali through Timbuktu to Gao and thence to Muli, which is in the country of the Limis and is the frontier province of the Mali empire. It continues from Muli to Yufi, one of the greatest countries of the black people, whose ruler is the most considerable of kings in the whole region. Yufi cannot be visited by any white man, for they would kill him before he got there. The Nile flows on to the land of the Nubians, who profess the Christian faith, and their capital Dongola (which has recently been given a Muslim sultan). Thence the river descends through the cataracts, which constitute the end of the territory of the black peoples, to Aswan in upper Egypt.'

Having travelled by river in both Egypt and Mali and gained intelligence about the 'forbidden' regions beyond, inhabited by Blacks or Christians or both, ibn Battuta perhaps regarded himself as an authority on these matters. But others in the 14th century knew well enough that the waters of Egypt derive largely from the highlands of Ethiopia (Habash); indeed the fear was expressed from time to time that the Christian rulers of that country had it in their power to divert the upper Nile into the Red Sea and to force Egypt into submission. This knowledge of an eastern source of the Nile encouraged the view of the Niger not only being separate from the Nile but also, despite ibn Battuta's testimony, flowing from east to west!

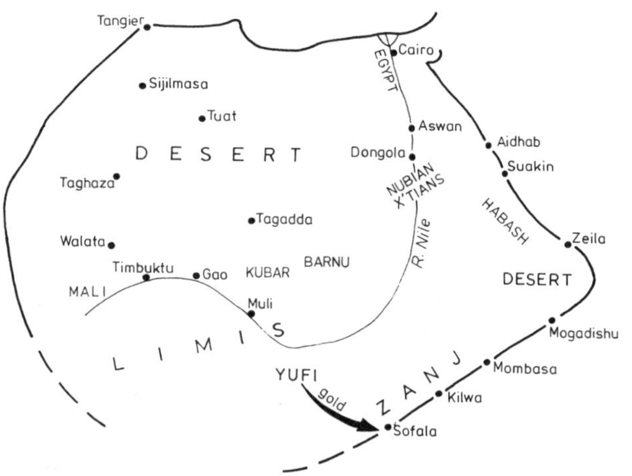

إن الله ناصر أمير المؤمنين الملك المنصور
الحسن بن سليمان وفقه الله تعالى وسد [د خطاه]

Verily God is the helper of the Commander of the Faithful, al-Malik al-Mansur [the conquering king] al-Hasan ibn Sulaiman, may Almighty God grant him success.

Inscribed 'al-Hasan (ibn) Sulaiman', who was sultan of Kilwa around 1320-33, this copper coin (2 cm diameter) was found during excavations at Great Zimbabwe in 1971. Though undoubtedly minted at Kilwa itself, where there is plentiful evidence of copper working at this period, the source of the metal was not local. Very probably it derived from Zimbabwe, copper being mined and refined, traded and transported in broadly the same way as was gold. (Photo, T.N. Huffman)

Kilwa and Zimbabwe in 1331

Ibn Battuta, the celebrated 14th-century traveller, sailed round the Horn of Africa to Mogadishu and then continued, crossing the Equator to reach the southmost limits of the Islamic world.

> After one night in Mombasa, we sailed on to Kilwa, a large city on the coast whose inhabitants are black. A merchant told me that a fortnight's sail beyond Kilwa lies Sofala, where gold is brought from a place a month's journey inland called Yufi.
>
> The city of Kilwa is among the finest and most substantially built in the world. Its sultan at the time of my visit was Abu'l-Mazaffar Hasan, surnamed Abu al-Mawahib (the Father of Gifts), renowned for his humility, generosity and hospitality. I saw at his court many sharifs from Iraq and the region of Mecca.

The passages from ibn Battuta's travels are based on H.A.R. Gibb's edition, published by the Hakluyt Society, vol. II, 1962, pp.379-82.

From the context Yufi can only mean Zimbabwe. But the name is based on a confusion arising from ibn Battuta's subsequent experiences in West Africa and the information he obtained in Mali. The real Yufi should have been in Nigeria. It was probably Ufe, nowadays spelt Ife, the early Yoruba capital which flowered at this very period: it sits on a small goldfield, and would have connected with the Mali empire through 'Muli', doubtless the Mande settlements around Bussa on the Niger river. Though an untiring traveller – the archetypal mediaeval hitch-hiker by sea and land – ibn Battuta was not much of a geographer, and mistook Zimbabwe for the same place approached from the other side of the Continent..

The *Kilwa Chronicle* preserves the full name of the sultan of Kilwa at this time – Abu al-Mawahib al-Hasan ibn Sulaiman, 'renowned for his generosity and courage.' He 'excelled in all branches of knowledge', having travelled in his youth to Aden and Mecca to study 'spiritual science'. He commemorated himself with an inscription (p.81) above a doorway in the palace of Husuni Kubwa (doubtless the 'court' where ibn Battuta claims to have been received in 1331). The discovery at Great Zimbabwe of a copper coin from the Kilwa mint bearing this same sultan's name nicely vindicates ibn Battuta's intelligence about the gold trade.

Husuni Kubwa palace at Kilwa, c 1300 AD: the ruins from the air, and Peter Garlake's axonometric reconstruction

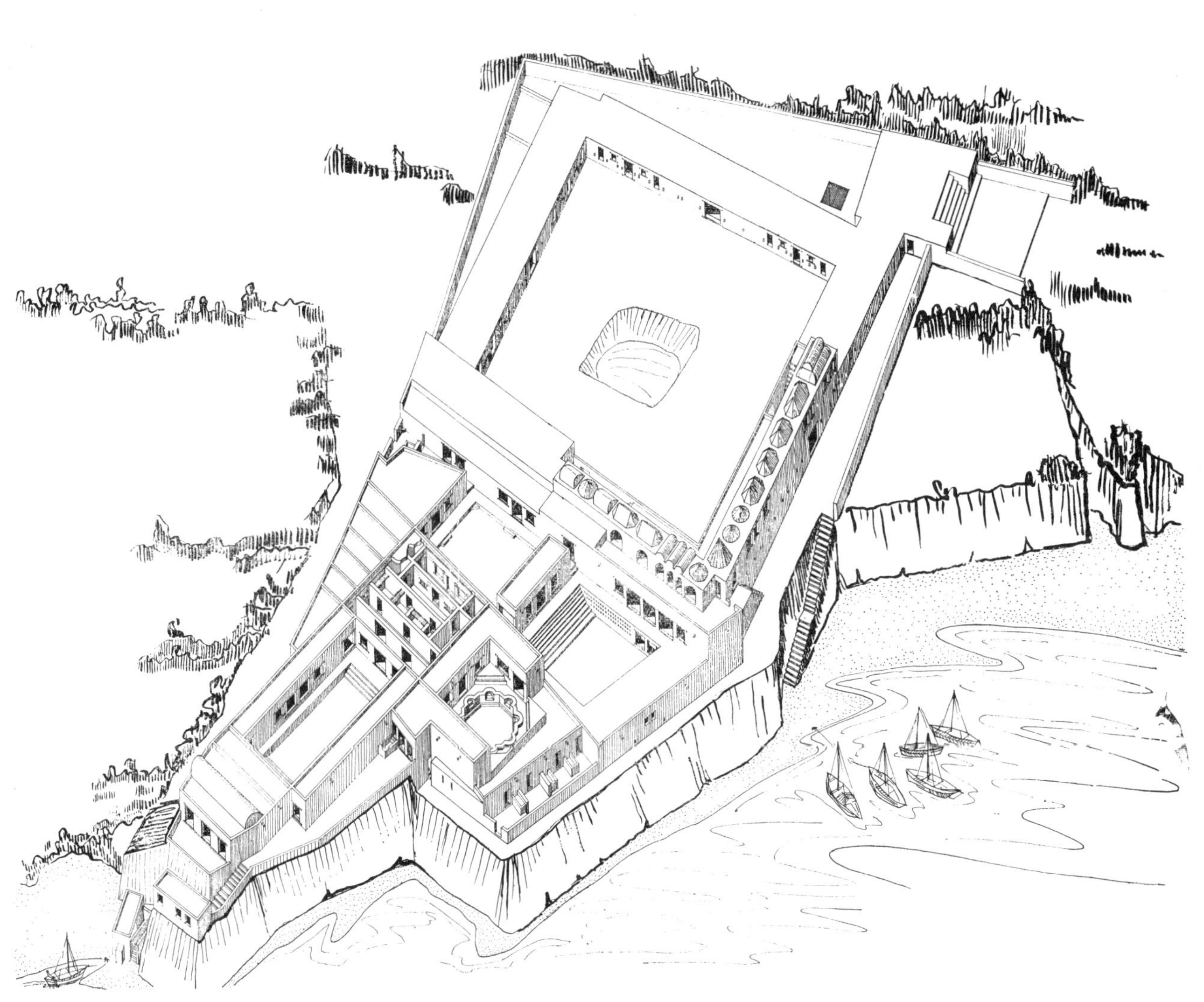

Husuni Kubwa

Built a mile distant from the town on a breezy cliff overlooking Kilwa harbour, this palace outshone in size and splendour any other in this quarter of the world. The unknown architect had obviously travelled and studied well; and as a result Husuni Kubwa at this southern extremity of the Islamic world combines an odd mixture of contemporary and archaic styles, some of the structures, forms and motifs being long obsolete in the Muslim heartlands. But other basic styles had been used for some time on the East African coast, as had also the coral masonry techniques distinctive of Swahili building. This suggests that the architect was native to the region or, if he was an expert attracted from overseas, that he delegated the entire practical side of the construction to the local masons.

Coup d'état

The sultan who commissioned Husuni Kubwa may have been the first of the Abu al-Mawahib dynasty, al-Hasan ibn Talut, who appears to have led a successful coup shortly before 1300 AD, just when international demands for gold were reaching unprecedented levels. The change of government seems to have been in two stages, the usurper coming forward as the strong man once the clique which had seized power proved inadequate for ruling the state. Chapter III of the Kilwa Chronicle, though difficult of interpretation on certain points, leaves strong hints between the lines:

> Then the throne departed from those who have been mentioned (the 'Shirazi' line of Ali bin al-Hasan) and the member of the house of Abu al-Mawahib (The Giver of Gifts) who succeeded was al-Hasan ibn Talut, who was celebrated for his intelligence and courage. With the help of his people he seized the kingdom by force; but as they were not strong enough to govern, he made himself independent of them, and seized the kingdom by violence. He reigned eighteen years and then died.

The Chronicle further testifies to the new dynasty's southern Arabian connection, and to the reputation, already noted, of al-Hasan ibn Talut's grandson, the sultan whom ibn Battuta met.

Hard times

After at most three generations, Abu al-Mawahib's successors abandoned Husuni Kubwa. Maybe the upkeep costs were more than they could afford, or than their subjects would tolerate. At the same time, as the Chronicle tells, they had difficulties in maintaining the great Friday mosque, no doubt for financial as well as merely technical reasons. Perhaps the price of gold slumped for a while, or Kilwa's monopoly of the Sofala route and the gold of Zimbabwe was not permanent or absolute. Again, it is worth remembering that this was the time of the Black Death which, whether it ravaged Kilwa itself or not, inevitably upset the conduct of international commerce. With reduced populations around a large part of the world, the demand for gold and other products of Africa would have eased. Whatever the explanation, the rulers of Kilwa moved to a more modest palace at the edge of the city, thus making themselves less remote from their subjects.

The news of this change of fortune at Kilwa quickly got around and caught up with ibn Battuta (as he continued his travels over the next twenty-odd years, to Delhi and China, Persia and Constantinople, Mecca and Alexandria, the Sahara and West Africa, and eventually home to Morocco):

> When the virtuous and liberal sultan died – may God's mercy be upon him – his brother Daud became ruler and conducted himself in the opposite manner. If a petitioner approached him he would say 'The giver of gifts is dead, and has left nothing to give.' Visitors would stay by his court a good many months and only then would he make them some small present, so that finally they gave up coming to his gate.

Kilwa could not remain forever a haven for poor scholars and itinerant sharifs.

Interpreting the ruins: a palace for commerce...

Peter Garlake's reconstruction of Husuni Kubwa (p.82) is based on a detailed architectural survey undertaken in 1962 alongside Neville Chittick's excavation of the ruins. The sultan's apartments, audience courts, domestic quarters and small ornate bathing pool (photos opposite) are easily distinguished. The big yard at the back was never properly completed: many of its small rooms may

have served as warehouses for the import and export merchandise which the sultan controlled. The pit in the middle of this yard – apparently a quarry for building material – remained unfilled.

The name *Husuni* is derived from an Arabic word meaning 'fort'; but this is a late and misleading description, since the building complex was never fortified. If this 14th-century palace had a special name, it has not survived. In its present ruined state it is called *Husuni Kubwa*, or 'the big Husuni', because of another structure, an open rectangular enclosure of similar date, adjacent to it. That is known as *Husuni Ndogo*, 'the little Husuni'. Superficially it resembles a fort, but the low walls and miniature bastions could not have been designed for serious military defence. Security does not seem to have been an overriding issue there and then (given the island situation). Perhaps the best guess is that Husuni Ndogo was built as a maritime caravanserai, under the shadow of Husuni Kubwa palace, for merchant-sailors from afar entering Kilwa's zone and the protection of the Abu al-Mawahib dynasty.

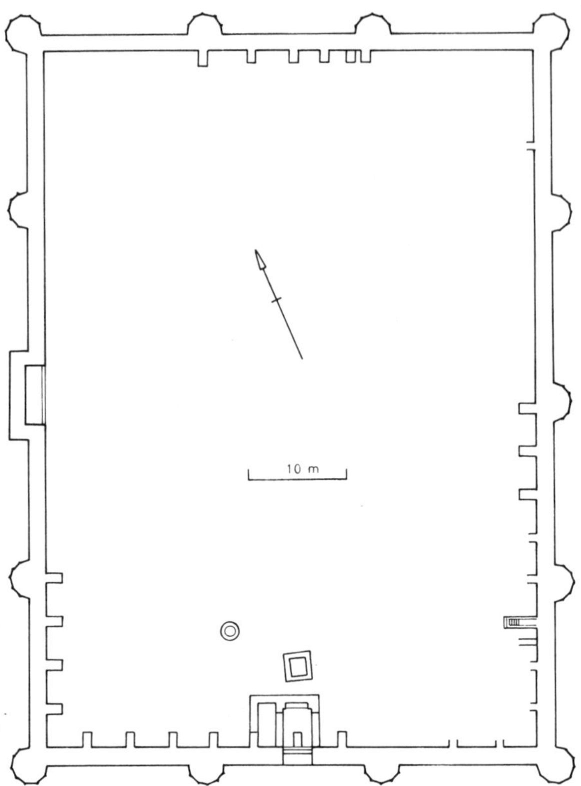

Husuni Ndogo (after Garlake). Excavations have revealed other buildings, whose purposes are poorly understood, in the interior. The north wall lies along the crest of the low cliff facing the harbour.

... in a kingdom by the sea

The reconstruction of Husuni Kubwa includes a miniature mosque on the shore below the northern staircase of the palace. Here one might briefly pray for a safe voyage, or conversely praise God upon successful return. This mosque is partly conjectural, half of the structure having been destroyed by the high tides (helped by a subsiding coastline) over nearly seven centuries.

But the moored ships are not conjectural. They are redrawn from those neatly scratched (perhaps as good-luck charms) in the wall-plaster inside Husuni Kubwa and on the outer wall of the Great Mosque (illustrations opposite). Such graffiti provide valuable evidence of the craft of the western Indian Ocean before the time of the Portuguese. Both square-rigged vessels, of the *mtepe* style with huge coconut-matting sails, and lateen-rigged *dhows* were sailing these seas. The latter belong broadly to the Arab tradition in the western Indian Ocean; the *mtepe* and its square sail by contrast are thought by some experts in nautical history to be part of the Waqwaq legacy. Its design of hull, as known from later examples, had its planks sewn together, not nailed; the same technique is recorded for building East African dhows of that period preceding the Portuguese contact.

There was of course a local iron industry, but it probably did not include nail manufacture on a large scale. Other techniques of joinery were employed instead, for domestic carpentry and boats alike. In particular, there was a developed craft in fibres, based especially on coir from coconuts, serving the needs of both the ship-building and the rigging. While the *mtepe* sails were woven from coconut-fronds, equally likely the triangular lateen sails for the *dhows* were made of cotton, for the growing of which the soils and climate of Kilwa are suitable. Here a cotton-cloth industry, always important in Islamic culture, is attested by the finding of numerous spindle-whorls. These were made of fired clay or often from rubbed-down pieces of broken pots, which are so plentiful all over the surface and beach of Kilwa Kisiwani after centuries of occupation (p.88).

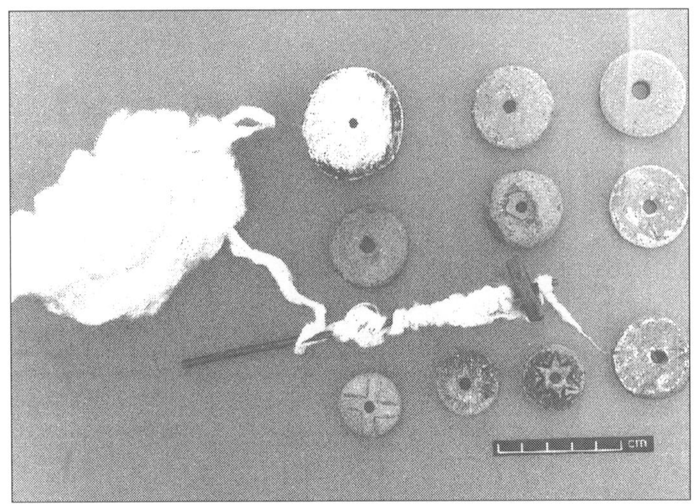

Spindle-whorls used for spinning cotton at Kilwa

Kilwa Kisiwani: the Gereza

In its present form this fort, standing on the harbour front, dates to the period of late Swahili revival and Omani expansion around 1800 AD (shortly before the main harbour and town of Kilwa were moved to the new site, Kivinje, on the mainland).

Closer examination reveals however that, with its late round corner towers (now partly collapsed), the Gereza encloses an older squarish building, doubtless the fort built by the Portuguese conquerors in 1505. That was abandoned in 1513 when the Portuguese found Kilwa to be of less strategic importance in the Indian Ocean than Mozambique Island to the south and their ally Malindi to the north. At the end of that century they moved their main base on the Swahili coast to Fort Jesus of Mombasa, which retained this role till its fall to the Omanis at the end of the siege of 1696-98.

The name gereza, *by which this Kilwa fort is known, usually means 'prison' in modern Swahili. It is one of the very few words in the language of Portuguese derivation—by a twist of meaning from* ingreja, *'a church'.*

Epilogue

Ancient Azania

It will be objected by some tiresome historians that the beginning of the story has not been told. True in a sense; for the 9th-century opening-up of the western part of the Indian Ocean – whatever one makes of the role of the Waqwaq – was not the first time that shipping connected the East African shores with the wider world. Eight-hundred years before that, when the Roman Empire was at its height all around the Mediterranean, ships from Egypt were sailing through the Red Sea and, mastering the behaviour of the monsoons, reaching both north and south India. A sideline of that traffic from Egypt and southern Arabia turned southwards at the Horn of Africa for trading along the 'Courses of Azania', that is the Swahili coast of later times.

Rhapta: a lost harbour

Of the several harbours of Azania, the most southerly

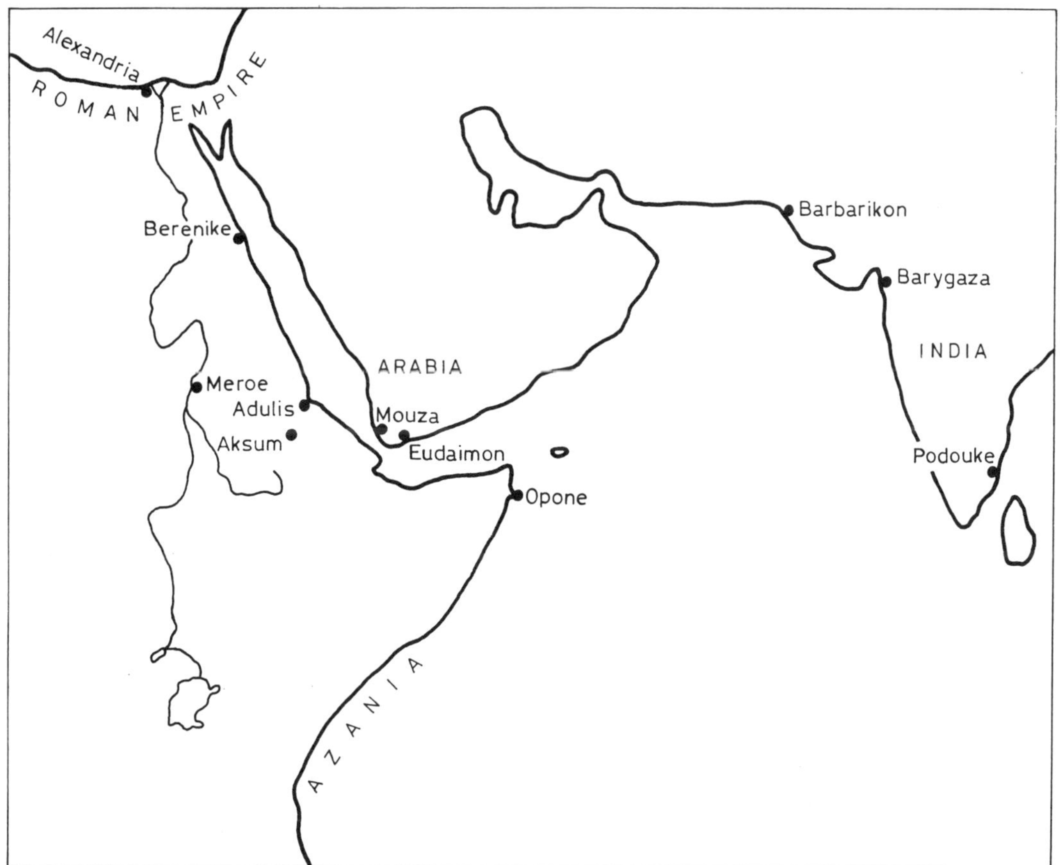

The Red Sea and Indian Ocean in the first century AD

and important was known to the Greek-speaking Egyptian sailors as Rhapta, 'on account of the small sewn boats'. These harbours are listed in Claudius Ptolemy's *Geography* written in the 2nd century AD. But more informative than that on the Red Sea and Indian Ocean is an anonymous document, also written in Egypt in Greek, but nearly a hundred years earlier. It dates probably to the reign of the Roman emperor Claudius or Nero, that is in the mid-first century AD, but reflects the information that had accumulated alongside commercial expansion since at least Augustus' consolidation of the Roman Empire and its control over Egypt some fifty years before. Known as the *Periplus of the Erythraean Sea*, this document provides remarkable details of sailing instructions, harbours and their import and export merchandise. It is the testimony of an intelligent eye-witness, whether a ship's captain, a commercial traveller or even an imperial trade official. The larger part covers the Arabian and Indian shores, but the first section systematically describes the African side of the Red Sea and Indian Ocean from Suez to this Rhapta, a place which has still to be located on the Kenyan or Tanzanian coast. Chapter 17 tells:

> There are brought to these marts of Azania things made specially in southern Arabia – spears, axes, small swords, awls and several kinds of glassware – and to some places wine and wheat, not really for trade but to gain the goodwill of the barbarians. Exported from here are quantities of ivory, though inferior to that of Adulis (the Aksumite port on the southern Red Sea), as well as rhino-horn, tortoise-shell and pearly seashells.
>
> Based on the Hakluyt Society's edition by G.W.B. Huntingford, 1980, and corrections advised by Professor Lionel Casson.

Not much more is recorded about these 'barbarians' save their tall stature and 'piratical habits'. For the author's purpose was to document not so much people as trade, the latter being regulated by captains sailing from southern Arabia who, for that purpose, 'know the native language'.

Although Ptolemy noted Rhapta as a 'metropolis', this was doubtless meant in relation to the lesser harbours of Azania. This statement has led some scholars to exaggerate the importance of what had been a regular harbour and the terminus of the long-distance shipping, but probably not much of a town. It must nevertheless have been sufficiently hospitable and developed to accommodate ships and their crews who had to sit out the turn of the monsoon, to repair their hulls and rigging, and to provision for the journey northward as far as the Gulf of Aden. Ptolemy's information – unlike that of the *Periplus* in the preceding century – was second-hand and already out-dated; if Rhapta was still functioning as an international trading station, it would have been past its prime. Despite searches, no archaeological sign of Rhapta or of the other harbours of Azania named in the

Periplus has come to light, while vague claims of finds of Roman coins on the Tanzanian, Kenyan and southern Somali shores should be treated with the utmost suspicion. If some day shipwrecks of that time should be located, their cargoes will have a lot to tell.

The nearest site at which pottery from the early Roman Empire and its trading partners has been found is Ras Hafun, right at the Horn itself (in north-eastern Somalia), the last point at which traffic from the Red Sea would set off for India on the monsoon. In the *Periplus* this place is named Opone. Here at least, as of course in India too, the testimony of this document is vindicated archaeologically.

Discontinuity

This commerce between Azania, the Red Sea and the Roman Empire with its eastern connection declined after the first century AD, the explanation for which has to be sought in the economic history of the world of late antiquity. Ironically for East Africa, it dried up just as agricultural iron-using people were about to settle towards the coast. Thus the supposition so often made that East Africa's later trade with the wider world and especially the Near East, described above, can be traced back to these pre-Islamic times looks, from all the information available, unfounded. Besides, when contact was made with the Islamic empire towards 800 AD, it was through the ports of Oman and the Persian Gulf, not the Red Sea. This break in continuity is borne out further by the history of the empire of Aksum in northern Ethiopia and of its political and economic involvement in the Red Sea, flourishing in early Christian times but fading and expiring in the late 6th and early 7th centuries, just when the Roman-Byzantine Empire lost control of the eastern Mediterranean and Egypt.

As far therefore as one can rest a case on negative evidence, the story is one of *dis*continuity through the middle part of the first millennium AD. This is not meant to imply a complete break in the population of the eastern African coastal regions: the brief allusion in the *Periplus* to the sewing of boats, a technique employed in later times, is one cultural detail suggesting the opposite, or at least a continuing tradition somewhere around the western side of the Ocean. Another item indicating some slender continuity of knowledge persists. The memory of ancient Azania seems to have been preserved as Zanj. Echoes of this old name for East Africa recur not only as seen in 'Zanzibar', but more subtly and recently in 'Tanzania', devised in the mid-1960s for the union of the islands with Tanganyika.

In historians' circles *Azania* is of course preserved in another way, having been chosen as the title of the journal of East African history and archaeology published annually since 1966.

Time and space

If then on the coast one can find in the Zanj of a thousand years ago an echo of Azania of twice that age, so too in the whole interior of eastern Africa could one trace back the history of agricultural and pastoral communities to the beginning of the Iron Age in the earliest centuries AD. In the interlacustrine region the adoption of iron, and the cultural and economic revolution which went with it, may date back further to the last centuries BC. This was a local facet of technological change affecting almost the whole of the Old World.

Continual change

In East Africa iron technology, and the grain-based agricultural settlement which it facilitated, radiated rapidly from that equatorial region of Lake Victoria and the Western Rift southwards and south-eastwards in the first few centuries AD. The hallmark of this new culture and economy was Bantu speech, which of course differentiated itself in time region by region, even district by district, as each of these agricultural communities settled successfully by adapting to the local ecology. As this process of expansion and settlement neared completion, towards 1000 AD – a thousand years ago more or less – we begin to pick up traces of more specific, indeed more specialised, regional cultures and ethnicities which have persisted till the present and form the subject of this book.

In the non-Bantu parts of East Africa – that is generally the northerly and drier north-easterly regions of Uganda and Kenya, as well as a broad area of grassy plateaus either side of the Rift in Kenya and northern Tanzania, as outlined in the middle section of the book – the early part of the Iron Age is more poorly understood. Here again it is in the *later* Iron Age, that is back to a thousand years ago, roughly, that we can trace and visualise existing or remembered peoples and their cultures. That must not be taken to imply stability through the millennium or simple tribal and linguistic continuity: one can demonstrate the opposite, by illustrating in particular the revolutionary impact of Maasai ways of organising the plateau grasslands and their cattle about three centuries back, and the infectious impact of the success and prestige of the pastoral Maasai minority. Alongside this the collapse of the irrigation-agricultural communities at Engaruka and elsewhere in the Rift remains strikingly clear on the ground though still inadequately explained. To the west, close to the Lake and in parts of eastern and northern Uganda, for another example, the expansion of Lwo might be seen not so much as migration and invasion as a movement of reform in settlement and land-use, in agricultural and pastoral efficiency.

The limitless past

This one-thousand-year concern is not meant to suggest that the history of pastoralists and cultivators before that time and even before the Iron Age are beyond the realm of historical research or are somehow 'irrelevant'. Similarly in Bantu regions, as just seen, the history of the populations can if one wishes be stretched back to the Bantu revolution based on iron technology and agricultural settlement of twice that age, and beyond that to the Late Stone Age populations, which were eventually largely assimilated or, should we say, Bantuized. From there we could extend our enquiries back any distance into the Stone Age and the history of man in Africa. But for the present purpose a concentration on the last one-thousand years only, looking back as explained to the middle of the Iron Age, is deemed sufficient. Over that period we can try to sense the 'personality' of East Africa and its parts.

Peoples and persons

It has been said, and said again so often, that the understanding of Africa's past is and will remain impoverished because the historical sources are limited, the evidence even then elusive and hazy. This is the 'dark continent' syndrome; and those who insist on maintaining a defeatist line will go on doing so. But for other continents too the sources for history are always limited, the evidence never perfect; what matters is to recognise and exploit the sources available and to devise ways of expanding knowledge through further search and enquiry. Still, it may appear to those brought up in the Asian and European tradition of History learning – characterised on occasion as 'all those kings and battles and things' – that much of African history and its sources remain impersonal, or rather 'personless'. For, while archaeological and linguistic research may inform us a lot about peoples and their cultures in the broad sense and, for more recent centuries, may provide their communal names, rarely do we meet here persons whom we may know by their individual names.

Names and meanings

But there are other sources which do tell us, often vividly, about individual persons of the last few centuries. For the second half of the nineteenth, descriptions are for some regions quite numerous and often objective; they include sketches and photographs of prominent and less prominent individuals. Before then however one relies largely on internal traditional accounts, the emphasis as one traces backwards being increasingly on kings, if not eventually legendary heroes or even gods, the ultimate concern being to demonstrate the impossible, the 'origin' of that line or kingdom.

But not all the names of kings and leaders are to be dismissed as mythical, as mere personifications of the hills and lakes, of thunder and rainbows. In the interlacustrine region the historicity of the king-lists of Karagwe and Nkore, of Bunyoro and Buganda and Rwanda, has been demonstrated in a way at periods eight or so generations back simply by cross-checking for references to wars and interactions between the neighbouring kingdoms. Such an exercise has however to beware of pitfalls; and one cannot insist that these accounts have been immune to simplication or manipulation. Indeed there is a suspicion that the very idea of a fixed king-list, that of arranging all remembered rulers of the past in an established chonological sequence, has been influenced by the introduction of literacy to the region in the 19th century and conversance with European and Biblical genealogies. But queries about the order apart, there are still a lot of names of real people who ruled in these regions and information on what they and their subjects achieved. Similarly in considering the southern Swahili coast, the temptation to dismiss the story of Ali bin al-Hasan of Kilwa as a typical foundation-myth has to be resisted in the light of the discovery of thousands of coins of the 11th century bearing his name. Maybe he did *not* come from Persia and maybe he did *not* literally buy the island for coloured cloth, but his memory was important enough to later generations so that a history was woven around his name. For another region again, the high lush cattle-pastures west of the Rift, who – and when – were Kipkoiimet and Kimnyike, individuals who left their mark in such a way to earn perpetual commemoration in the cycle of age-set names?

The founders

We may be less convinced about Mbega and his career progressing from an uncouth hunter of bush-pigs to becoming king in Usambara. Or again about the Chwezi 'dynasty', from which some of the later interlacustrine ruling lines claim descent. These stories and their variants are not simple falsifications; they have an obvious historical purpose, and meaning too, even if they lend themselves to disputed interpretations. Contradiction is of course all part of their purpose, sufficient to ensure the survival of such traditions and their rival versions.

Among the more famous foundation stories are those told on the north side of Lake Victoria, in Buganda and Busoga, relating to Kintu. More than one version is admitted in the standard history of Buganda composed at the end of the 19th century by the prime-minister, Sir Apolo Kaggwa. This book, literally 'the kings' (*Basekabaka*), begins typically at the beginning, and thus runs from the first, Kabaka Kintu, to the thirtieth, the powerful Mutesa I who died in 1884. Of this Mutesa there is good independent documentation, including that of Speke who visited his court close to modern Kampala in 1862. Several of his predecessors in this list of thirty kabakas, probably most of them, were very real kings and persons. But Kintu himself is obviously a problem. The name looks to be cognate with *omuntu* for 'man', the singular of *(a)Bantu*, 'people'. (It should thus correspond to *mtu* in north-eastern Bantu languages such as Swahili, and to the *muntu/bantu* form found all the way from South Africa to equatorial Gabon.) Whether then Kintu, the man or the idea, relates to all mankind or just a particular people becomes a moot point. Translated as Adam, the question of person or personification is no nearer solution.

Equally interesting are some other king-lists of Buganda, recorded over the last one-hundred years, from the time of the early Muslim and Christian contacts. These give Kintu the alternate name of Ham, that is, as one of the three sons of Noah, the first African.

Adam's ancestors?

Perhaps unfortunately, some later historians of Buganda, inspired not only by Kaggwa but also by rival histories of the kingdoms to the west of Buganda with their claims to a legitimate descent from an ancient Chwezi period, have tried to trace the Ganda line back beyond Kintu. By diligent searching of traditions, especially at burial shrines, they have identified his royal ancestors – the antecedents of Adam so it would seem.

Well, not quite. For Mr Charles Kabuga (writing in the *Uganda Journal*, vol. 27, 1963), Kintu's ancestry runs back a few generations – via a Kabaka Buganda – to

> the first kabaka who was called Kabaka Muntu, and his Nabagereka (consort) was Kibaawwo. God put them in the village called Nnagalabi, on Budo hill.

Here we have the unequivocal Adam, and Kabuga's account, modelled on the Book of Genesis, runs on: 'These are the children of Kabaka Muntu and his Nabagereka...', over twenty of them, who were given various territories round and about. From one of these the kingship passed through a succession of sons, grandsons and their brothers to Kabaka Buganda, the father of Kintu.

Here the purpose of Kabuga's contribution comes clear: it is 'to confirm that Kabaka Kintu was born in Buganda', was a real son of the soil, in opposition to Kaggwa and other authorities who would have him arrive from the east or some other direction. In a sense he did, because, as Kabuga adds, Kintu had in his youth been driven out of his native country by a usurper and regicide – by name Bemba, which others interpret as 'snake' – only to return later to avenge his father and claim his royal inheritance.

And the proof of it all could, in 1963, be found at Entebbe, 'behind the present Police Station', where Kabaka Buganda had his capital and was also buried. His grave and shrine were being attended by a priestess; 'the jaw bone is still preserved and the barkcloths are still intact.' Even then it was a minority cult and tradition, 'hardly known', as Kabuga admitted.

Not surprisingly, few non-Baganda intellectuals have been very excited by these 'discoveries', and many Ganda authorities too have been sceptical. Most of the claims of this sort should probably not be dismissed as complete fantasy; they may in part serve as a necessary attempt to marry the independent sets of traditions of the different elements, the senior clans, which have made up the Baganda people. The later strength of the monarchical tradition has resulted in parallel genealogies being combined and rolled out as a single extended line.

The Land of the Moon

Places or regions are commonly, as here, named after peoples, or rather the two may signify very much the same thing, culturally and geographically at the same time. Explaining the meaning of such names is a favourite antiquarian pastime frequently involving downright linguistic manipulation and scholarly delusion. But even a dubious derivation, once enshrined in local tradition, can become significant and may inspire new enquiry. How else does one explain Richard Burton's infatuation with Unyamwezi, 'the Land of the Moon' (*mwezi* being 'moon'), which at the same time he found to be the 'garden of Central Africa'? Reaching that country from the east in 1857 along the foot-portered caravan-route, he was perhaps entitled to meditate and eulogise. One thing on his mind was the allusion of the ancient geographer Ptolemy to the 'mountain of the moon' from whose snows, some then supposed, the Nile had its source. But more immediately, while convalescing at Tabora, far from any high mountain or great river, he was enthralled by Unyamwezi's 'peaceful rural beauty', its neat villages dispersed among 'well-hoed fields', with 'frequent herds of many-coloured plump humped cattle', and 'mingled flocks of goats and sheep', as well as rice ripening in the swamps. Covering the distance as he did from the coast opposite Zanzibar to Lake Tanganyika (already so named), Unyamwezi, approached after the early rains, was as idyllic as any spot along that well-trodden road; it was a land of moderation, contrasting not only with 'the red glare of barren Ugogo' which he had just crossed to the east, but also with the 'dark, monotonous verdure' of the regions beyond. Burton did not, as his companion Speke did, divert northwards to see the shores of Lake Victoria and witness the more luxuriant, intensively cultivated and densely populated districts of the East African interior.

In the days of the grandfathers of the grandfathers...

But being observant, inquisitive and intelligent – albeit not always balanced in his descriptions or unbiased in his judgements – Burton got a feel of Nyamwezi history. Although he found it 'broken up into petty divisions, each ruled by its own tyrant', he learned that in the 17th century Unyamwezi had been 'united under a single sovereign'; the last of these 'emperors' died 'in the days of the grandfathers of the grandfathers' of those with whom he spoke. Later research has corroborated in fair part, but not in perfect detail, this testimony of an ancient Nyamwezi empire. The idea may be exaggerated, but it should help explain what clearly struck Burton's mind, the remarkable continuity of this single Nyamwezi language over a wide area, stretching moreover as far north as Lake Victoria to include Usukuma – which means just that, the northern side.

Burton's reading and thinking went further:

> Travellers in Africa in the seventeenth century concur in asserting that, between 250 and 300 years ago, there was an outpouring of the barbarians from the heart of Aethiopia and from the shores of the Central Lake towards the eastern and southern coasts of the peninsula, a general waving and wandering of tribes which caused great ethnological and geographical confusion, public demoralisation, dismemberment of races, and change, confusion, and corruption of tongues. (*Lake Regions*, II, p.5.)

Such a 'catastrophic' view of African history may read rather oddly now, well over a century after. It was perhaps the ethnologists and geographers, not so much the people of Africa, who were then 'confused' and 'demoralised' by the sheer amount of information about the interior of the continent which was rapidly becoming available and needing to be organised, let alone interpreted. And Burton himself had not yet unmuddled his own mental map, containing a vague concept of 'Aethiopia', or Black Africa, and still a 'Central Lake', something which he, with Speke's help, was then disproving to European readers, by substituting for this old idea the mapping of several separate great lakes. But Burton could at least see the historical message to be derived from the body of ethnological and linguistic observations which he and others were accumulating. Though he was far out on the dating and misconceived about the dynamics, he was recognising the historical fact of the Bantu expansion from equatorial to southmost Africa.

Penetration: commercial, scientific and political

It did not need such British travellers as Burton and Speke in the 1850s to link the Lake regions with the coast, or again Thomson in the 1880s to prove that it was possible to reach the nearer side of Lake Victoria by traversing the highlands and the Rift and the Maasai grasslands instead of skirting round their southern edge. They were following well-worn routes about which there was already plenty of intelligence available in Zanzibar and Mombasa. Burton's importance nowadays lies in what he observed and recorded about people and places, markets and merchandise, in particular in Unyamwezi and the Lake Tanganyika region. The same applies to Speke and Grant who went northwards through the interlacustrine zone, to Stanley who continued westwards to penetrate the Congo basin, and Livingstone whose travels between the 1840s and 1870s ranged from South Africa as far as Tanganyika and Tabora. Their diaries and books provide a vivid supplement to the internal historical sources for the 19th century.

More immediately of course their impact in Europe was both intellectual and political, some of the writings, of Livingstone and Stanley in particular, being put to definite propaganda purposes in missionary or imperialist circles. But even the more scientific recordings had the effect of drawing the continents closer. In this sense they foreshadowed the more formal annexation of East Africa by European powers in the 1890s, that is Germany in the south and Britain, expanding from its old connection in Zanzibar, to the north, the region comprising Uganda and Kenya.

Local and international

So, looking back to the first section of this book and the safaris of Burton and Stanley along the trade-routes in the second half of the nineteenth century, the commerce in salt, ironware and foodstuffs which they observed at local and regional levels was in no way new. What *was* new then was the scale and pulse of change as the connections with more distant regions, which included the coast and the world beyond the seas, became more direct and obvious. As seen, the foreign explorers and the Christian missionaries who followed soon after were not the cause of this, but they illustrate the expanding economic and cultural tentacles penetrating what Stanley, a journalist by profession, called 'dark', even 'darkest', Africa.

Pressures and initiatives

In this situation the established social and political institutions, let alone market regulations and norms of informal exchange, were strained to keep apace. For with the increased demands for both ivory and slaves, and the imports of firearms to facilitate the capture of both, opportunities for quick profits from such exploitation of natural and human resources threatened to outweigh the advantages of stable settlement and cultivation. Thus in some regions the development of long-distance trading and international involvement, even if essentially indirect, undermined the local economic infrastructures which had been essential for their initial success. Perhaps the worst examples of social collapse occurred in the Congo basin well beyond the great lakes; yet many parts of eastern Africa as well felt the strains keenly, and in places the scars have barely healed even now.

But that is only one way of seeing things. In general the local infrastructures held, or rather adapted constructively. Right through the 19th century one can trace the developing involvement, efficiency and sense of identity of those who controlled the trade-routes and pioneered new ones – notably Yao from Lake Nyasa down to Kilwa and the other southern Swahili harbours, Nyamwezi along the 'central' routes between Lake Tanganyika and the Zanzibar coast as well as south-westwards to Katanga for copper among other products, and Kamba through the Mombasa hinterland to the highland edges. New demands were placed on manufacturing, and not only on smiths to supply modern weapons in profusion. For instance, one broad class of import in special demand was cotton cloth; and as this outstripped supply, in certain regions up-country cotton was grown, spinning learned and weaving looms set up. In several places in southern Tanzania the sites of these 19th-century weaving workshops have been

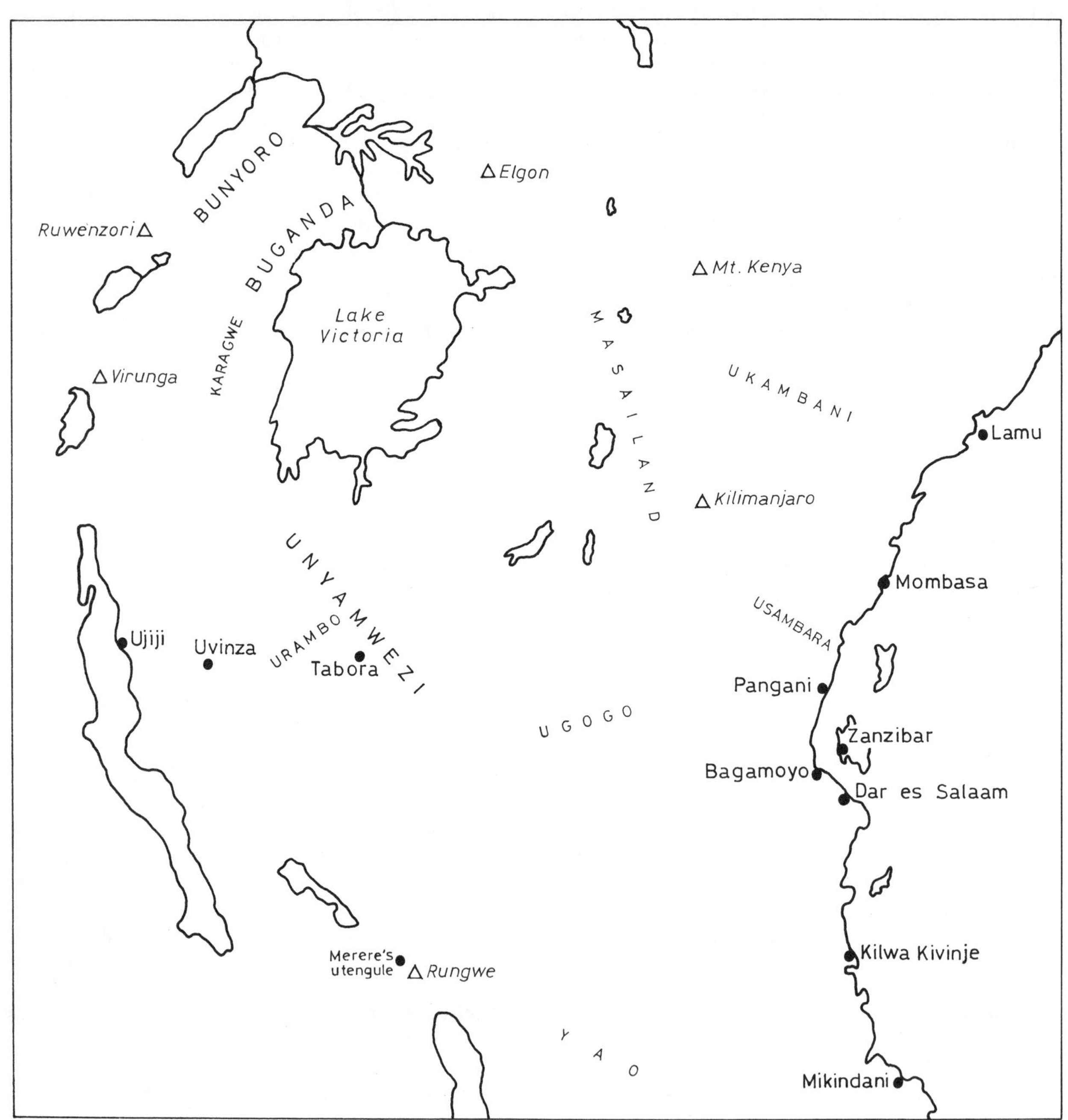

Nineteenth-century East Africa: regions and towns mentioned

A Safwa cotton-cloth weaver and his loom photographed about 1900 in the southern highlands of Tanzania. (F. Fülleborn, Das Deutsche Njassa- und Ruwuma-Gebiet, *1906.)*

*Fifty years earlier Burton saw similar looms in Unyamwezi (*Lake Regions, *II, p.1)*

remembered with pride. Intermediate technology has its own history.

Old kingdoms adapt....

The African reactions during this half-century before formal European take-over were remarkably varied. Some of the old interlacustrine kingdoms were sufficiently organised and adaptable to put the changing situation to their own profit. In Buganda, the king and the administrative corps, both at the court and in the districts, turned the new opportunities for obtaining wealth into increased patronage and bureaucratic efficiency. Internally there was more competition for education and for the rewards which went with it, especially as literacy was introduced. Thus new elites emerged, alongside the structural changes and modernising trends within the continuous tradition of an ancient kingdom.

Comparable developments, if on a lesser scale, are detectable in Karagwe and Bunyoro, while near to the coast in the Usambara highlands and their adjacent lowlands agriculture was intensified, sometimes with irrigation, to provide for the markets on the caravan routes as well as to supply the islands of Pemba and Zanzibar. There the growth of a plantation economy, geared for export crops (cloves especially) for overseas markets and dependent on servile labour, created a loss in self-sufficiency and the need to import food from the mainland, to feed freemen and slaves alike.

...... while upstart empires blossom and fade

In much of central, southern and western Tanzania small chiefdoms had been the norm whose rulers, try as they might, could not rival the power, prestige and length of genealogies of the interlacustrine ones. Now many of them endeavoured to exert themselves economically and militarily and to dominate their neighbours. We have observed the example of the rival chiefdoms of Uvinza. Such expansion was rarely permanent; there were built-in destabilising factors.

Among these were the *rugaruga*, bands of armed men initiated into a blood-brotherhood under particular leaders, and sometimes enlisting mercenaries from more distant parts into their numbers. Increasingly these professional armies required firearms and supplies of ammunition, or at least an elite corps so equipped. Certain historians argue that the *rugaruga* began in central Tanzania

Outside the abandoned fortifications of the utengule *of Merere near Mbeya (photo from Fülleborn).*

as a development from, or a reaction to, the incursions in the mid-nineteenth century of Ngoni hordes from the south who introduced a diluted form of Zulu weaponry and regimental techniques. Be that as it may, the sudden appearance of *rugaruga* from the 1850s onwards has to be seen in the rapidly changing economic and political context of this period. Traditional chiefdoms needed them, whether for raiding, for enforcing tolls (*hongo*) from caravans, or for their own security as the situation around them changed. To survive one had to exploit, by fair or less fair means, on a scale sufficient to satisfy one's followers and clients, but for the same reason in a way to ensure the continuity of production and of trade passing through one's area.

Temporary capitals and military headquarters

Some of these leaders fortified their headquarters as a way of defence against these new military tactics and firearms, and at the same time to serve as recognised centres of their government and of the trade which they were trying to both attract and exploit. A few of these capitals, especially in southern Tanzania, remain visible archaeologically, in certain cases as impressive historical monuments. One such is that of Merere, the Sangu leader, established in the 1870s close to modern Mbeya.

Especially spectacular were the mushroom empires of Nyungu-ya-Mawe around Ukimbu, itself an unattractive and sparsely populated region lying between Usangu and Unyamwezi, but with important trade-routes on all sides, and of the better-known Mirambo to the north. Though both these leaders claimed to be of chiefly descent, their empires were their personal creations, dependent on the loyalty and efficiency of their *rugaruga*, and their ability to lead or send wide-ranging terror campaigns when needed. Toughness was the order of the day – aptly signified by Nyungu-ya-Mawe's name meaning the 'stone pot', that is the unbreakable one.

Mirambo, Tippu Tip and the Vinza salt-kings

Mirambo's sphere, as it has been mapped, was as extensive as Nyungu's. But it was the nuclear area of western Unyamwezi – called appropriately Urambo – lying between Tabora and Uvinza, which was essential to his success from the 1860s to 1880s. Here he could control

Sir Richard Burton, scholar and traveller, as painted by Lord Leighton (National Portrait Gallery). Brought up in an English colony in France (barely before the wounds of Waterloo had healed), Burton later rebelled from Oxford and joined the Indian Army, where the combination of his intellect, his keen perception of people and places and his contempt for convention proved a constant thorn. From the 1850s to 1880s he travelled in East and West Africa and elsewhere, with the unique achievement of visiting both Mecca and 'the City of the Saints', the Mormon settlement at Salt Lake in Utah. His literary works include a translation of the Arabian Nights, *while the books describing his travels and observations in East Africa remain indispensable historical sources, in particular the* Lake Regions. *(The standard modern biography of Richard Burton is that of Fawn Brodie:* The Devil Drives *1967; while a brief picturesque account of his East African exploration is given by Alan Moorehead in* The White Nile *1960.)*

Mirambo, from the photograph taken in 1882/3 by Rev W.G. Willougby of the London Missionary Society (by kind permission of the Council for World Mission)

all the trade to and from Lake Tanganyika and the new regions of intense exploitation in the Upper Congo basin beyond. That was the sphere of Hamed bin Muhammed, the Zanzibari merchant-traveller better known as Tippu Tip (on account of his reputation in deploying firearms). As the latter tells in his Swahili autobiography, he found it politic to maintain a pact with Mirambo. In this way he managed, throughout the years of exploiting the deep interior, to keep open his supply-lines with Tabora, the Swahili-Arab up-country base in Nyamweziland, and thus with Zanzibar.

Among the constant minor annoyances on the road from Tabora to Ujiji, the port on Lake Tanganyika, were the size of tolls exacted by the salt-kings of Uvinza, both Ruzunzu of whose local power Stanley (as described above) was made aware in 1876 and his successor Kasanula. Tippu Tip regarded the Vinza as extortionate and treacherous in the extreme. On his way eastward in 1881 he found their behaviour especially obnoxious. His version of the encounter runs as follows:

> Nilipofika Uvinza wakatughasi Wavinza, sultani Kasanura akataka mahongo bila kiasi. Nikampa akatunyang'anya watumwa mia u khamsini. Akatoka mtumwa wetu katika kambi, hachukuliwa wakauawa watu wangu Wanyamwezi wanne, hapana hoja iliyo yote. Mimi haazimu kupigana, naye Said bin Sultan akaniambia haifai afadhali kustahamili, maana tuna pembe nyingi, na watoto tulio nao haifai kupigana. Haona, ndio maneno yake Said bin Ali. Nikakubali zilla hata tukatoka katika inchi ya Uvinza, hata tukawasili Tabora bisalama lakini taabu kuu iliyotupata.
>
> On reaching Uvinza we were harassed by the locals, and their chief, Kasanula, who demanded an excessive toll. I gave in to him and he stole from us 150 slaves. One of them escaped from the camp and four of my Nyamwezi were taken from me and killed, for no justifiable reason. I decided to attack, but Said bin Sultan advised against it, counselling patience, as we had with us a great quantity of ivory and the youngsters with us were not experienced in fighting. I saw the wisdom of Said's words and agreed. We left Uvinza and reached Tabora safely, though not without difficulties.
>
> *Maisha ya Hamed bin Muhammed el Murjebi yaani Tippu Tip kwa maneno yake mwenyewe*, edited and translated by W. H. Whiteley (East African Literature Bureau, 1966, p.94-5).

A few months later Tippu Tip returned, with Mirambo's connivance, to teach these Vinza a lesson. This campaign, and the siege engine employed to eventually break Kasanula's defences, must have been costly. It did not smash the Vinza or wrest their control of the salt production, but it did mean the installation of a more compliant chief. That of course was no lasting solution from an outside angle: Mirambo had done just that a few years before Tippu Tip. Uvinza's natural resources and strategic position had always to be reckoned with. In the long run each party needed the other.

The Napoleon of Central Africa

By this stage the image of Mirambo as a bandit leader was being replaced by one of respectability, because of his success in enforcing a measure of stability over the general disorder and ensuring the smooth passage of trade. It was Stanley who, encountering Mirambo twice in the 1870s, on the first occasion in conflict, on the second in friendship and making blood-brotherhood, made the journalistic comparison with Napoleon. But this vast empire, rather like Napoleon Bonaparte's not long before it in Europe, lacked institutional roots, and barely survived Mirambo's death in 1884.

Yet his memory has survived; and the *rugaruga* spirit, disciplined, militant and independent at the same time, has in a way been revived and institutionalised on occasion. A modern historian of that region, Fr John Kabeya, recalls how in 1961 he made a pilgrimage to the sites of Mirambo's headquarters or palaces (*ikulu*). Their remains were still visible, though rather hidden in the bush, for in the intervening years the district had been depopulated (by government policy, because of sleeping-sickness) and had become the abode of giraffes and elephants, of rhinos and buffaloes. It required some imagination to envisage these places as the centre of an empire only three generations previously. At Mirambo's grave where, it is said, a commemorative stone had been erected some years before, it was found that those who still feared or hated his memory had come later and destroyed the monument. History is sometimes just too close for modern comfort.

But on a more positive note John Kabeya could document cultural continuity from that day to this. A Nyamwezi melody which 19th-century *rugaruga* had adopted for a marching-song with a subtle if unmistakably militant message –

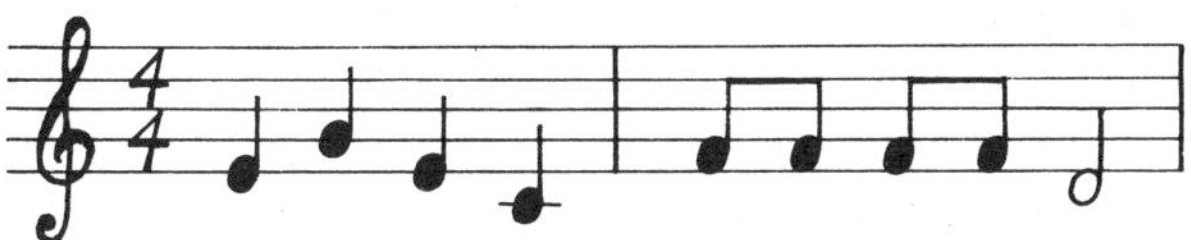

Uhuu! Chuma chabela mitwe
('We smashed their heads with iron weapons'—or a boast to that effect)

was heard by Mwalimu Julius Nyerere in 1962, the year after Tanganyika's independence, at a Youth League convention in Tabora. This tune was thought worthy of being preserved for posterity. Put to the ruling party's song *TANU yajenga nchi* ('TANU builds the nation') and quickly popularised by radio, not only in Tanganyika but equally in Kenya with the simple change from *TANU* to *KANU*, it has become an East African cultural hallmark.

The foregoing paragraphs are based on J.B. Kabeya's book *Mtemi Mirambo* (1966, in East African Literature Bureau's 'Wananchi Mashuhuri' series), especially pp.i-v (*Dibaji*), and 15-16.

Reading East African History

Detailed bibliographies of East Africa, its history and archaeology, may be found in the more comprehensive works and the original and thematic studies noted below. Here only a guide to some of the more useful literature is attempted.

Background and general reference are provided by the collaborative eight-volume *Cambridge History of Africa* (1975–86) and the UNESCO *General History of Africa* (1981–). The latter, broken into shorter chapters written by a larger number of authors, is less consistent, but is valuable for the range of approaches it tries to encompass.

More integrated coverages of African history exist, notably the Penguin *Short History of Africa* of R. Oliver and J.D. Fage (1962, with several subsequent revisions), and *African History* by P. Curtin, S. Feierman, L. Thompson and J. Vansina (1978). The various books of Basil Davidson, beginning in 1959 with *Old Africa Rediscovered*, have done much to inspire new enquiry with the effect, of course, of requiring revision and amplification.

For East Africa specifically: B.A. Ogot and J.A. Kieran (eds.), *Zamani: a survey of East African history* (1968, rev.1973); and R. Oliver and G. Mathew (eds.), *(Oxford) History of East Africa*, vol. I (1963). The latter in particular is superseded by subsequent research which it was designed to stimulate and which this book attempts to assimilate. *Zamani* includes a key to ethnic and linguistic classification which is followed here.

A number of important regional studies are included in the collections edited by A. Roberts, *Tanzania before 1900* (1968); I.N. Kimambo and A.J. Temu, *A History of Tanzania* (1969); B.A. Ogot, *Kenya before 1900* (1976); and J.R. Gray and D.B. Birmingham, *Precolonial African Trade* (1970). The results of the materials collected about the same period by the wide-ranging 'History of Uganda' project at Makerere have not all been published. Some however are mentioned below, and there are useful papers in J.B. Webster, *Chronology, Migration and Drought in Interlacustrine Africa* (1979).

These general and collaborative works illustrate the range of sources – linguistic, ethnographic, archaeological, oral and documentary – from which the history of eastern Africa is researched and reconstructed.

Iron Age archaeology is covered in D.W. Phillipson's *Later Prehistory of Eastern and Southern Africa* (1977), and in more up-to-date but summary fashion in his *African Archaeology* (1985). Much of the research of recent years is reported in *Azania*, the journal of the British Institute in Eastern Africa, published annually since 1966.

From 1960 moreover the *Journal of African History* (Cambridge U.P.) has carried articles describing new research findings, as well as summaries of the progress of archaeological work and radiocarbon-dating results.

For geographical introduction, see W.T.W. Morgan, *East Africa* (1973), and *East Africa: its peoples and resources* (1969) for broader background.

The Lake Regions and deep interior

General introductions may be found in the works referred to, especially Roland Oliver's chapter in *Cambridge History of Africa*, volume 3, followed by E.A. Alpers and C. Ehret in volume 4.

Among the histories of interlacustrine kingdoms, both older texts and later interpretations, the following are important:

- Bunyoro: J.W. Nyakatura, ed. G.N. Uzoigwe as *Anatomy of an African Kingdom* (1973).
- Buganda: M.S.M. Kiwanuka, *History of Buganda* (1971); A. Kaggwa, *The Kings of Buganda* (1901, ed. Kiwanuka, 1971).
- Ankole: S.R. Karugire, *A History of the Kingdom of Nkore* (1971).
- Rwanda: J. Vansina, *L'évolution du royaume Rwanda des origines à* 1900 (1962); L. de Heusch, *Le Rwanda et la civilisation interlacustre* (1966).
- Burundi: E. Mworoha, *Histoire du Burundi* (1987).
- Karagwe: J. Ford and R. de Z. Hall, in *Tanganyika Notes and Records* 24 (1947); I.K. Katoke, *The Karagwe Kingdom* (1975).
- Kiziba: F.X. Lwamgira, *Amakuru ga Kiziba n'Abakama bamu* (Bukoba, 1949; unpub. trans. E.R. Kamuhangire).
- Busoga: D.W. Cohen, *The Historical Tradition of Busoga* (1972).

A critical review of the oral sources and their published versions and of chronologies derived from them is attempted by D.P. Henige, *The Chronology of Oral Tradition* (1974). Iris Berger, *Religion and Resistance: East African kingdoms in the precolonial period* (Musée royal de l'Afrique centrale, Tervuren, 1981) is an important essay in modern interpretation. Some of the considered thinking of both Berger and Henige is contained in their essays in J.C. Miller's volume, *The African Past Speaks* (1980), which with its introduction constitutes a valuable critical reassessment of oral sources and their historical use.

Lake Victoria Nyanza itself, and trans- and circum-lake historical themes, especially as they relate to the eastern shores and islands, are addressed by G.W. Hartwig, *The Art of Survival in East Africa* (1976), which concentrates on Ukerewe in the 19th century, and by M.G. Kenny, 'The Stranger from the Lake' in *Azania* XVII (1982).

For the Lwo and their impact, and the north-easterly borders of the interlacustrine zone:

- northern Uganda and Sudan: J.P. Crazzolara, *The Lwoo*, esp. part 1, 'Migrations' (Museum Combonianum, Verona, 1950); J.M. Onyango-ku-Odongo and J.B. Webster, *The Central Luo during the Aconya* (1976).
- south-eastern Uganda and western Kenya: B.A. Ogot, *History of the Southern Luo* (1967).
- Teso: J.B. Webster et al., *The Iteso during the Asonya* (1973).

On royal insignia, symbolism and ironwork, see H. Sassoon in *Azania* XVIII (1983), and F.L. Van Noten, *Les tombes du roi Cyirima Rujugira et de la reine-mère Nyirayuhi Kanjogera* (Tervuren, Museé royal de l'Afrique centrale, sciences humaines 77, 1972) describing unparalleled materials obtained by excavating in Rwanda. Further archaeological investigation of this subject, concentrating on north-western Tanzania, is set out in P.R. Schmidt, *Historical Archaeology* (1978). For background to iron and its technology, see relevant essays in R. Haaland and P.L. Shinnie, *African Iron Working – ancient and traditional* (1985).

Archaeological investigations of Bigo are reported in *Uganda Journal* by P.L. Shinnie, XXIV (1960), and M. Posnansky, XXXIII (1969). Ntusi is mentioned in *Azania* V (1970) and XX (1985); new work there, and also at Mubende Hill and Munsa, in the late 1980s is to be published by the British Institute.

On salt in East Africa, its sources, preparation and trade, and archaeological investigations of saltworks:

- Ivuna: B.M. Fagan and J.E. Yellen, *Azania* III (1967).
- Uvinza: J.E.G. Sutton and A.D. Roberts, *Azania* III (1967).
- Kasenyi and Katwe: E.R. Kamuhangire in *Hadith* 5 (Nairobi, 1975).
- Kibiro: J. Hiernaux and E. Maquet, *L'âge du fer à Kibiro* (Tervuren: Musée royal de l'Afrique centrale, sciences humaines 63, 1968).
- Sindo (Kaksingiri): M.G. Kenny, *Azania* IX (1974).

See also D. Morgan's survey in *Tanzania Notes and Records* 74 (1974).

Industries, trade and agricultural and pastoral production generally are discussed in a broader theoretical perspective in *An economic history of Kenya and Uganda, 1800–1970* by R.M.A. van Zwanenberg with Anne King (1975). R. Austen's *African economic history* (1987) is different not only in its continental coverage but also in its more varied theoretical concerns.

The highlands, eastern Rift Valley and adjacent plains

Besides the coverage provided in the general histories and volumes of essays mentioned, the results of historical-linguistic research undertaken in this region have been enlightening for cultural and economic history alike. See especially C. Ehret's contribution to Ogot's *Zamani* and his monograph *Southern Nilotic History* (1971); also relevant essays in Ehret and M. Posnansky, *The archaeological and linguistic reconstruction of African history* (1982). Some of these deal with time-depths much longer than that of this book. As argued however in reviews in *Azania* (VII, 1972 and XIX, 1984), some of the dating of cultural and ethnic developments based on linguistic criteria alone may be exaggerated.

The present author's *Archaeology of the Western Highlands of Kenya* (B.I.E.A. Memoir 3, 1973) addresses the history of a broad region, and in particular the study of the Sirikwa. For further investigations, and a reconsideration of Kalenjin and Maasai history, see the article on 'Hyrax Hill and the Sirikwa' in *Azania* XXII (1987).

For Engaruka and irrigation agriculture in the Rift and northern Tanzanian highlands, see articles in *Azania* I (1966), XIII (1978) and XXI (1986); and the special volume of *Azania*, XXIV for 1989, on the broader context of agricultural technology, field systems and their history.

Among oral-historical studies of specific peoples and regions, the following are noteworthy: I.N. Kimambo, *A Political History of the Pare* (1969); G. Muriuki, *A History of the Kikuyu* (1974); W.R. Ochieng', *A Pre-colonial History of the Gusii* (1974); G.S. Were, *A History of the Abaluyia* (1967); and for the south-eastern end and coastal hinterland with a treatment of the Mbega myth, S. Feierman, *The Shambaa Kingdom* (1974). For the cultural history of Kilimanjaro and the Chagga people, see G. Philippson's linguistic study, *Gens des Bananeraies* (1984).

Together with Ogot's pioneering work on Lwo history noted above, these researches, mostly pursued in the 1960s, illustrated the feasibility of local historical enquiry in regions lacking both written documents and strong and long monarchic traditions (as exist in the interlacustrine zone). Even then it is noticeable how pastoral (or pastorally inclined) societies tended to be neglected by the new schools of History, or to be left to scholars with an anthropological background, well aware though several of these were of the new historical interests. A number of valuable research efforts are summarized in the volumes of the Kenya Historical Association, *Hadith* (ed. B.A. Ogot, 1967–79). For a published monograph on the 'pastoral' non-Bantu north, the most specifically historical example is J. Lamphear's *Traditional History of the Jie* (1976).

The distinction between historical and anthropological approaches is now considerably eroded, especially with the current concern for ecological understanding which draws on the findings of diverse disciplines as well as undermining the old division between the colonial and pre-colonial past. Several essays in D. Johnson and D. Anderson, *The Ecology of Survival* (1988) illustrate this: especially important here are those by Anderson and by R. Waller on the reactions of Maasai-speaking groups to the crises around the turn of this century. The ecological history of parts of Maasailand is further illustrated by Waller and R. Lamprey in Peter Robertshaw's *Early Pastoralists of south-western Kenya* (B.I.E.A. Memoir 11, 1990), a volume which concentrates however on pre-Iron-Age pastoralists some two-thousand years ago.

For other regions too, there is a substantial body of ethnographic and social-anthropological literature written over the last one-hundred years. Outmoded though a lot of this is in outlook, the materials documented remain of inestimable value for modern historical study; references may be found in the works cited above, and in the several volumes covering most of East Africa in the *Ethnographic Survey of Africa* series of the International African Institute.

G.P. Murdock's *Africa: its peoples and their culture history* was at the time (1959) a bold attempt to organise the accumulated anthropological information and to correlate it with comparative linguistics for broad interpretation of cultural and economic development in recent millennia, thus combining an old-fashioned ethnographic obsession with an imaginative historical approach. It can be faulted on detail, and some of its exciting hypotheses have not withstood closer examination. It remains useful for reference, nevertheless, and for its stimulating way of tackling cultural and linguistic diversity, as along the Bantu borderland. A more recent exposition of methods of historical reconstruction is *Kenya's Past* by T. Spear (1981). Concentrating on the central and south-easterly part of that country, this book successfully disregards the old historiographical gulf between the coastal region and the interior of East Africa.

The Coast and the wider world

The historiography of the East African coast itself is frequently characterised as divided into two schools – an old 'imperialist' one, typified in outlook as well as scope by R. Coupland's *East Africa and its Invaders* of 1938 (a book little used these days), and an 'enlightened' school which puts the emphasis on the indigenous Swahili population and local initiative. But while grosser reactionary attitudes have been superseded, there has never been much of an intellectual debate, concerned though some recent writing has been to explain its stand. The issue has been further confused by uncertainty on how to handle the Islamic factor, whether to regard it as essentially 'foreign' or 'African', and how to recognise an Arab (or even 'Persian') element both in recent centuries and in 'mediaeval' times.

For the development of the Swahili coast and its harbour-towns in relation to the Indian Ocean up to the 16th century and the period of Portuguese intervention, Neville Chittick's chapter in volume 3 of the *Cambridge History of Africa* is a good survey, if a bit old-fashioned and superseded by the latest archaeological work and dating. A useful short account is that of D. Nurse and T. Spear, *The Swahili: reconstructing the history and language* . . . (1985); while a volume entitled *From Zinj to Zanzibar: studies in history, trade and society on the eastern coast of Africa* (Paideuma, 28, 1982, edited by J. de V. Allen and T.H. Wilson) contains a range of information and ideas.

Horn and Crescent by R.L. Pouwels (1987) is a study of Swahili cultural, intellectual and Islamic history from the 9th to 19th centuries.

For a survey of coastal archaeology, James Kirkman's *Men and Monuments on the East African Coast* (1963) is told rather discursively, and arranged not by periods but geographically from north to south. It is fuller on the Kenyan stretch of coast and summarises the results of his earlier research publications on Gedi and other sites; these are now overtaken on dating and other details by the work of Chittick and Garlake and later still of Horton. A more recent conspectus appears in Graham Connah's *African Civilizations* (1987); while R. Fischer's *Korallenstädte in Afrika* (Oberdorf, 1984) is a well illustrated account for the Deutschefon public.

Chittick's excavations at *Kilwa* and *Manda* are published by the British Institute as Memoirs 5 (1974) and 9 (1984) respectively. The Shanga excavations of Mark Horton are to be published in the same series. Memoir 1, published in 1966, is P.S. Garlake's *Early Islamic Architecture of the East African Coast*, which was a thorough study for its time and remains a work of basic reference. Revisions to the architectural and archaeological chronology before 1300 AD are adumbrated in the article by Horton and numismatic colleagues on the Mtambwe hoard in *Azania* XXI (1986).

Other archaeological and architectural surveys and excavations of Swahili sites, from the Comores to southern Somalia, are reported in *Azania* and in publications of the Tanganyika/Tanzania Antiquities Department and of the Kenya Museums (notably the reports of T. H. Wilson, 1978 and 1980); also J. de V. Allen and Wilson on houses and tombs of the northern coast in *Art and Archaeology Research Papers*, December 1979.

The archaeology of the 17th century and its international contacts has been treated rather separately and from a less indigenous angle, concentrating on Fort Jesus of Mombasa and the underwater study of the wreck of the Portuguese ship 'S. Antonio de Tanna' sunk in front of the Fort during the siege in 1697. The latter has yet to be fully written up; but see H. Sassoon in *Azania* XV1 (1981) and the exhibition in Fort Jesus Museum. The architecture of the Fort and the excavations conducted there are reported in James Kirkman's *Fort Jesus* (B.I.E.A. Memoir 4, Oxford, 1974).

For the international context, some of the essays in H. N. Chittick and R.I. Rotberg, *East Africa and the Orient* (1975, but based on a conference in Nairobi in 1967) remain useful for scholarly reference. For the gold-trade factor and *Great Zimbabwe*, see Peter Garlake's book of 1973 and more recent interpretative attempts summarised in Connah's *African Civilizations*. Portuguese involvement in the Indian Ocean is told by C.R. Boxer, *The Portuguese Seaborne Empire* (1969). The interaction between coast and interior is handled in the *Cambridge History of Africa* volume 5 by A.C. Unomah and J.B. Webster, followed up in volume 6, for the late 19th century, by A.E. Atmore and Marcia Wright.

Later Swahili history and its broader context are covered, with differing emphases, by C.S. Nicholls, *The Swahili Coast* (1971) and Abdul Sheriff, *Slaves, Spices and Ivory in Zanzibar* (1987).

An extremely useful anthology of written texts and documents relating to the coast was edited by G.S.P. Freeman-Grenville and published by Oxford in 1962 as *The East African Coast: select documents*. Scholars needing original or critically annotated editions can find the references there.

Acknowledgements

It was mentioned at the beginning that this book represents a cooperative endeavour over many years. The responsiblity for its contents rests nevertheless with the author who needs to acknowledge certain specific debts incurred.

Sources of quotations are mentioned in the text: authors, editors and publishers are thanked for readily agreeing to requests. In particular I must mention Dr G.S.P. Freeman-Grenville and Oxford University Press for the quotations from the Kilwa Chronicle and other documents relating to the coast; also the Uganda Society for those on the Chwezi on p.6-8; Kenya Literature Bureau (on behalf of the old E.A.L.B.) and the Hakluyt Society for use of various pieces; and Arthur Probsthain of London for allowing the 15th-century illustration of the giraffe taken to China to be copied from the cover of J.J.L. Duyvendak's pamphlet *China's Discovery of Africa* (1949).

Several colleagues have kindly supplied photographs as noted in the captions. The rest are from my own and the British Institute's collections, some of Kilwa being taken by the previous Director, the late Neville Chittick, others by myself while assisting him in 1962. That of the Kilwa coin found at Great Zimbabwe (p.81) was supplied by Tom Huffman. The aerial photograph of part of the Engaruka fields (p.35) is reproduced by kind permission of the Director of Tanzanian Surveys and Mapping; and the other aerial view, that of the Bigo earthworks (p.7), attributed to the late Gervase Mathew O.P., by courtesy of Basil Davidson – whose inspiration over these years may be recognised through the different sections of this book. The photograph of Mirambo (p.99) is reproduced through the cooperation of the Council for World Mission. I am especially indebted to Hamo Sassoon, whose varied work is drawn upon in the three main sections, especially for the photographs of his excavations in the Engaruka villages (p.37), and for the account of Bweranyange and king Ndagara's blacksmithing feats told in Azania XVIII, on which I have drawn (p.21). The plans of coastal architecture are derived, directly or indirectly, from those of Peter Garlake, whereas for the latest discoveries on the coast and their historical significance I have benefitted from talking with Mark Horton up to the time of going to press.

I am very appreciative of the encouragement to persevere with this book received from the Governing Council of the Institute. Moreover every member of the Institute's staff has contributed to its production since 1986 when the travelling exhibition began to be planned and the challenge it presented was gradually realised. I must mention in particular the typing of drafts, revisions and insertions by Naomi Mariwa, the sober editorial comments offered by Eva Ndavu, the patient photography of specimens and their printing by Simon Reuben Ndambuki, and especially the successful labours of Gilbert Oteyo in producing the maps, plans and other line-drawings to fit the text.

The other artistic contributions – on p.5, 20, 53, 69 and 90 – are by the hand of Spaña Davison, who very kindly volunteered her skill just when it was needed, accepting also the challenge of the Sirikwa Hole reconstruction (p.51). This last is based on a model, interpreting the excavation results from Hyrax Hill and other sites, which was prepared for the exhibition by an artist, Avril Sadler, with practical assistance in the claywork from my wife Inez. The musical score (p.101), being one line from the *rugaruga* chant recorded by Fr John Kabeya, was transcribed by my daughter Tamar. It should of course run on, by alternating between the leader and the troop, line by line, indeed page by page – but this book, unlike the timeless *rugaruga* spirit, had to end there.

J.E.G.S.

Index

Memoirs of the British Institute in Eastern Africa

The following volumes, each representing a substantial contribution to research on eastern African history and archaeology, are available through booksellers. Members of the Institute are entitled to a one-third discount by ordering through the Institute's Nairobi or London office.

3. **The Archaeology of the Western Highlands of Kenya**
   by J.E.G. Sutton — £9.50

4. **Fort Jesus: A Portuguese Fortress on the East African Coast**
   by J.S. Kirkman — £9.50

5. **Kilwa: an Islamic Trading City on the East African Coast (2 vols)**
   by Neville Chittick — £42

6. **The Prehistory of Eastern Zambia**
   by D.W. Phillipson — £16

8. **Culture History in the Southern Sudan: Archaeology, Linguistics and Ethnohistory**
   by John Mack and Peter Robertshaw — £15

9. **Manda: Excavations at an Island Port on the Kenya Coast**
   by Neville Chittick — £25

10. **Excavations at Aksum: research at the ancient Ethiopian capital by the late Dr Neville Chittick**
    by Stuart Munro-Hay — £30

11. **Early Pastoralists of south-western Kenya**
    by Peter Robertshaw — £26

Azania

AZANIA is the principal journal covering the precolonial history, archaeology and related studies of eastern Africa. It has appeared annually since 1966. It carries contributions from a wide range of scholars in East Africa and numerous other countries. Contributions should be addressed to the Editor, *Azania,* Box 30710. Nairobi.

AZANIA is obtainable through booksellers or by membership of the Institute. Current annual subscription rates are £12.50 for individual membership; £30 for corporate membership.
All back volumes are available, with generous reductions for runs and complete sets. Enquiries and orders should be addressed to the Membership Secretary, B.I.E.A., Box 30710, Nairobi or the London Secretary, 1 Kensington Gore, London, SW7 2AR.